A FIELD GUIDE TO
FEEDER BIRDS
EASTERN AND CENTRAL
NORTH AMERICA

THE PETERSON FIELD GUIDE SERIES®

A FIELD GUIDE TO
FEEDER BIRDS

EASTERN AND CENTRAL NORTH AMERICA

ROGER TORY PETERSON

Maps by

VIRGINIA MARIE PETERSON

SPONSORED BY
THE NATIONAL WILDLIFE FEDERATION AND
THE ROGER TORY PETERSON INSTITUTE

HOUGHTON MIFFLIN COMPANY
BOSTON   NEW YORK

CONSERVATION NOTE

Birds undeniably contribute to our pleasure and standard of living. But they also are sensitive indicators of the environment, a sort of "ecological litmus paper," and hence more meaningful than just chickadees and cardinals to brighten the suburban garden, grouse and ducks to fill the sportsman's bag, or rare warblers and shorebirds to be ticked off on the birder's checklist. The observation of birds leads inevitably to environmental awareness.

Help support the cause of wildlife conservation by taking an active part in the work of the National Audubon Society (950 Third Avenue, New York, NY 10022), the National Wildlife Federation (1412 16th St., N.W., Washington, D.C. 20036), The Nature Conservancy (4245 North Fairfax Dr., Suite 100, Arlington, VA 22203), and your local Audubon or Natural History Society. On the international level, don't forget the World Wildlife Fund (Suite 800, 1601 Connecticut Ave., N.W., Washington, D.C. 20009). These and other conservation organizations merit your support.

Library of Congress Cataloging in Publication Data
Peterson, Roger Tory, 1908–1996
A field guide to feeder birds, eastern and central North America /
Roger Tory Peterson ; maps by Virginia Marie Peterson.
p. cm — (The Peterson field guide series)
"Based upon A field guide to the birds, Fourth
edition, ©1980 by Roger Tory Peterson" — T.p. verso
ISBN-13: 978-0-618-05944-7
ISBN-10: 0-618-05944-X
1. Birds — North America — Identification. 2. Bird feeders — North America. 3.
Birds — Food — North America. I. Title: Feeder birds. II. Peterson, Virginia Marie, 1925–
III. Peterson, Roger Tory, 1908-1996 Field Guide to the birds. IV. Title. V. Series.
QL681 .P45 2000
598'.097—dc21   99-053956

Photo Credits
Roger Tory Peterson: vi, 17, 101 left, 101 right
Richard Day/Daybreak Imagery: ii–iii, 4, 5, 6 left, 6 right, 8 left, 11 left, 12, 22
Jeff Milton/Daybreak Imagery: 8 right, 11 right

Consultant on text: Dr. Noble Proctor
Consultant on maps: Paul Lehman
Consultant on overview: Pete Dunne
Based upon *A Field Guide to the Birds,* Fourth Edition,
© 1980 by Roger Tory Peterson.

Book design by Anne Chalmers

Printed in the United States of America
DOW 20 19 18 17 16

CONTENTS

INTRODUCTION

One of my fondest memories from early childhood is of watching birds come to the backyard feeding station. There was always an electric feeling when a new species showed up and out came the Peterson Field Guide in an attempt to identify the bird. The feeders were not elaborate, but the enjoyment was one of the formative aspects of my birding career.

We had a feeding tray mounted atop a post and a large round circle below it that was cleared to the dirt and edged with bricks. Wide open for the ground feeders to not only find food but to allow unhindered vision for safety from predators. My dad was always experimenting with various bottle feeders, and he created a rather inventive method of feeding suet in an enclosed aluminum container that the woodpeckers and nuthatches could access only from the bottom and that thwarted the Starlings. This creativity with the feeding station was even more special when we saw the success each adaptation brought. In the winter, swirls of Common Redpolls would arrive to feed in the circle and Evening Grosbeaks covered the feeding tray, looking like festive Christmas decorations against the snow.

Therefore, the die was cast at an early age. Birds, natural history, and biology would be the focus of my life. My career would find me roaming the world studying birds and leading birders to all continents. However, the simple pleasure of feeding and watching birds in my backyard remains. Each year I still generate a list of the species that visit the feeders. On the now too few cold winter days when Redpolls or Evening Grosbeaks visit, their arrival takes me back to those days of wonder that got me started.

Today, I am joined by more than 80 million people in America who watch and feed birds. Birding is one of the fastest growing outdoor — as well as indoor — activities. The so-called backyard birder has now become a vital link in the overall understanding of birds, bird behavior, and range expansion. Many winter rarities, more often than not, are detected at someone's bird feeder and reported to the birding community. In several instances these sightings have been the first steps of advancing bird populations. I well remember spending 8 hours glued to a window at a feeding station in Connecticut before a Red-bellied Woodpecker showed up. One of the first ever seen in the state, it was a precursor to the onslaught that has made the species the most common woodpecker in the southern Connecticut woodlands. In the 1950s a Tufted Titmouse at a feeder was a red-letter day, and House Finches were unheard of. Indeed, they were not depicted in the earlier Peterson Field Guide, and, therefore, when this introduced species to the East Coast began to expand its range, it was often mistaken for a Purple Finch. It was the bird-feeding stations that marked the start of the population explosion of these and other species.

Today, feeder records are often used as test sites to determine food preference at feeding stations. In addition, winter bird counts are more accurate when feeders are observed for a full day, and the arrival dates of many species are best indicated by records of feeding stations. The bird feeder, then, has had an impact not only on birds and the people who love to look at them but also on the scientific community. We have come a long way in the last 50 years.

This book has been designed to help backyard birders by combining Roger Tory Peterson's illustrations of the birds most likely to be seen at feeders with text modified specifically for those who have bird-feeding stations. Each plate includes information on not only identification and ranges, but on preferred food and feeder types. Also included is a checklist with spaces for species, date and time seen, and comments. Over the years you may be surprised by how regularly birds return to the feeding site, and the anticipation of their arrival will enhance your enjoyment of feeding birds.

So spread the book open, fill up the feeders, and keep an eye on the comings and goings of the birds; it will be a lifelong hobby!

—*Noble Proctor*

BIRD FEEDERS

The variety of bird feeders available is staggering. Nearly a half billion (yes billion) dollars are spent on bird feeders and nesting boxes each year in the U.S., ranging from the basic flat tray to elaborate triggered mechanisms that exclude unwanted bird species or that combat the ultimate warrior in the bird-feeder wars, the gray squirrel.

Location and Cover: Of First Importance

The establishment of a bird-feeding station can be as simple as casting bird seed on the ground. This is sure to bring success, although it may be limited to pigeons, House Sparrows, and starlings. Feeding on the ground, however, can be a very important aspect of a bird-feeding station that attracts the widest variety of species. Some birds will feed only on the ground; others will never come to the ground.

When placing a feeder, you will naturally encounter some restrictions. Certainly, you want to have a good view of the birds coming to feed. A spot easily seen from a window is often the first choice.

Consider, also, an area that is advantageous for the birds. While feeding, a bird is in a vulnerable position. Its attention is focused on food and in many feeders, the view is obstructed. Therefore, the bird will quickly obtain a seed, look around, then eat it. If you have an active feeding site, the chances for a sneak attack by a cat or bird of prey is decreased because usually one of the feeding birds is looking for predators while another is feeding. Once the danger is spotted and the alarm call given, the feeder can empty in unbelievably short order. Although birds can leave a feeder quickly, it is of no value if they must cross a large open area before reaching shelter. Try to place the feeder where shelter can be reached quickly. Next to a dense bush or shrub, a brush pile, or even near an obstacle where the birds can slip around a corner from view when they're being chased. This may be enough to hinder the predator's view and allow the birds to escape. If at all possible, do not place a feeder where there are large windows on two or three of the sides (such as in an alcove) as this can be deadly when a predator attacks. When startled, a bird's natural reaction is to head for any type of cover. If that cover is reflected in a window, the bird may fly into the window and upon impact be either killed or stunned, a perfect scenario for the attacking predator, who now swoops in to claim the victim.

While nearby shelter is essential, keep in mind that it can also be used as cover by predators. With ground feeders, any cover close to the site could shelter a stalking cat and be much more of a detriment than a help to the birds. A tall shrub or tree too close to an upright feeder may be just what a hawk can use for an ambush. Many times I have seen a Sharp-shinned Hawk sitting in a bush next to a feeder just waiting for the birds to become complacent about its presence. In an instant it darts from the bush, and with the short distance to travel the feeding birds have no reaction time. It is obvious, then, that placement of feeder to cover is very important for success. Six feet between the bird feeder and the nearest cover is a good rule of thumb. If the feeder is closer to cover, some birds can sense the danger and will stay away. If you are not having luck attracting birds to your feeder, evaluate the cover predators can use, and if the cover is too close, move the feeder.

Feeder Types

GROUND

Ground feeding can be done in several ways. Scattering seeds directly on the ground is the simplest and will work; however, there are a few drawbacks.

1. The husks of sunflower seeds are poisonous to grass and will kill all the grass in a heavily seeded area. You must clean up such sites each spring to prevent grass loss.
2. The birds must search for the seeds, which leaves them open to predator attack. This method is also less likely to attract timid species that prefer to simply drop down to a site where the food is obvious, grab a seed, and go.

Ground feeders can attract species that are reluctant to go up to pole or hanging feeders. Cardinals often prefer to feed on the ground. The raised wooden edge keeps seeds from spilling out.

4

3. It can be difficult to clean away the buildup of unwanted seeds. This can lead to overfeeding or—worse—a moldy buildup of rotted seeds that can introduce noxious fungi into the birds' systems.

Given these drawbacks, it is best to clear an open area for ground feeding. This can be done simply by keeping the grass cut low around the feeder base or ringing an area with edging and clearing it down to the dirt. It will eliminate the three problems listed above. The area can be a ring, or a square, or whatever shape you wish. Scattering the seeds evenly over the area rather than concentrating them in one spot will allow a variety of species to feed. All birds have a specific "approach range," which varies from species to species. Redwing Blackbirds allow a very close approach, and many will feed in a tight feeding area. Mourning Doves, on the other hand, allow an approach of only a foot or so, and anything within that range gets a quick flick of the wing. Cardinals are notorious for keeping their distance from one another while feeding. If the area is small and does not allow an approach range of at least 3 feet, you will usually have only one pair of cardinals visiting the site. If it is larger, however, several pair can fit in a zone that allows ample spacing. A friend experimented by continuing to spread seed over a large ground site until he was getting 12 pair of cardinals feeding at one time. The drawback was that the area covered some 30 feet by 30 feet and he had to scatter buckets of seed each day to attract them! The key is to keep it open, scatter food evenly, and keep it clean.

TABLE OR TRAY FEEDER

A table feeder is any flat surface up off the ground. It can be a tray atop a post, a flat piece of plywood placed across the corner of deck railings, a flat board atop cinder blocks, or any variation on that theme. You may want to consider putting a protective lip around the edge to keep seed from blowing away or being scratched off. To make cleanup easier, adapt one end with a wing nut so that the protective lip can be swung open and excess seed swept off. Another method is to leave an opening of 3 inches or so in one of the side bars. If the seed becomes soaked and mushy with rain use a hose to flush the seed out through the opening.

A simple feeding tray that is easy to fill and maintain. A wide variety of species enjoy feeding where visibility for predators is unobstructed.

Two of the most popular feeders. The shelter feeder (left) protects the feeding area from rain and snow to some extent. Open on all sides, it allows for excellent visibility. Hanging feeders (right) have become the standard in feeding stations. They are easy to fill and attract a wide variety of species.

One interesting adaptation of table feeding I have seen was the placement of a shallow roof gutter along the entire edge of a deck railing. This "trough" was filled with seeds and cleanup was a simple flushing of the gutter with a hose. Table feeding allows a variety of species to visit. Species such as Evening Grosbeaks that find it difficult to cling to hanging feeders choose the feeding tray. Even ground feeders may learn to come up and feed on these open trays after a while.

POLE FEEDER

Next to hanging feeders, the classic slant-roofed square feeder atop a post is the most popular feeder sold. It lost its position as feeder of choice when the "army of the squirrel" took over the free-meal program of backyards.

A pole is so easy for squirrels to climb that a large flange is a must to attempt to deter the pole climbers. These flanges come in many shapes, sizes, and connecting mechanisms. Some flanges have been designed to tilt when a squirrel jumps on them, so that the squirrel is tossed to the ground. Special poles have also been designed specifically to thwart squirrels from getting up to the feeder. Pole feeders should be placed at least 6 feet away from anything a squirrel might jump from to reach the feeder.

FLY-THROUGH

All sides of this feeder are open for easy entrance and departure. Many birds require this openness before they will enter a roofed structure to feed. Basically a tray with four corner posts and a slanted roof, it is one of the easiest feeders to construct. Its size is limited only by your imagination. I have seen massive 4-foot-square feeding houses with more than 20 birds feeding in it at once!

ELF-FEEDER

Because of the problems with squirrels at pole feeders, automatic feeders were designed. A bin of seeds is made available to the birds when they land on the feeding bar at the base. It is designed to open via a counterweight on the rear of the feeder. The mechanism can be set for the weight of various species, from Blue Jays to House Finches. The extreme weight of a squirrel triggers the mechanism to close. Others are open all the time until the "heavyweight" squirrel arrives and the feeding slot closes.

ANGING FEEDER

Hanging feeders are the most commonly used types of feeders. They are available in many forms, shapes, and sizes. The commercial products usually consist of a tube or series of tubes with openings that have a perch at the base. Some of these self-feeding tubes can hold a remarkable amount of seed, so they need refilling less frequently. This continuous supply can be a boon to the Evening Grosbeaks and House Finches that spend the entire day sitting at a feeder. When choosing a feeder be sure the holes are surrounded by metal protective collars. Sooner or later most squirrels will get to these feeders, and holes without the metal protection are easy for them to chew open. Hanging feeders are also made to hold specific food types. Thistle feeders, with small openings for thistle seeds, are the delight of goldfinches. Peanut butter feeders can be made by simply drilling large shallow holes in logs and filling them with a peanut butter and seed mix. Poles hung with upturned nails can hold orange halves, which attract orioles. Jars with openings in the caps and suspended by wires and filled with seeds are a great favorite, as are the simple feeders made by cutting openings into plastic soda bottles. The options are limitless.

Note: To eliminate the dominance of species such as starlings at both pole and hanging feeders, encasing the feeder in small-hole chicken wire or turkey wire can make it an exclusive site for titmice, chickadees, and other small species that can enter through the screen opening. Larger species won't be able to fit through. The only drawbacks are the appearance of the wire encasement and the difficulty of working out a screening modification that is far enough away from the food so that larger birds cannot stick their heads in and reach it.

UET FEEDER

During the winter months many birds prefer to feed on fats such as beef suet. Nuthatches and woodpeckers will visit chunks suspended in old onion bags or special string-bag suet feeders.

Melted suet with seed mixed in and allowed to harden in holes drilled in a short piece of birch log can be a great attractant. Special wire mesh baskets allow ready access to the formed blocks of suet and seed that are available. Coconuts with a quarter section cut away create an easily suspended cup that can

The hanging log feeder (left) is easy to make. Holes drilled in a short log, then filled with melted suet or a peanut butter/seed mixture will attract woodpeckers, chickadees, titmice, and nuthatches. Hummingbird feeders (right) are very popular. Their bright colors and sugar water attract Ruby-throated Hummingbirds in the East. Keep your eyes open for rare hummingbirds in the late fall.

be filled with suet and seeds, and eventually even the white coconut will be pecked away. One caution in using suet is that in warm weather, this beef product can turn rancid and provide a feeding site for many unwanted insect species. You may want to use meat products only in the coldest weather.

NECTAR FEEDER

Commercial hummingbird feeders have become one a stalwart of the backyard feeding station. Many kinds of plastic and glass feeders are available. Bright red in color, they vary greatly in shape and size. Filled with sugar water, a hummingbird feeder can provide hours of enjoyment once the hummingbirds find it. They will often return with their young and introduce them to the bounty.

A spinoff of the hummingbird feeder is the oriole feeder. It uses the same sugar water mixture, but the colors are usually bright orange and it has larger perches for the much larger orioles. One clever adaptation is feeder port regulation via a perch interconnection. The hole stays closed, thereby thwarting bee entry, and when the oriole lands on the perch, the hole to the nectar opens.

Remember: Bees can be a problem at these feeders so the commercial types often come with bee guards. In the heat of the summer you will need to clean the feeder out about twice a week with a mild bleach solution, let it dry, and refill it. Failure to do so is asking for the solution to ferment and enhance the growth of a black fungus that can harm the orioles.

FOOD

The types of food that can be put out to attract birds are almost as limitless as what we eat. It is amazing to see what birds will feed on, from old pork chops to spaghetti! Here we will deal with the foods most often used to attract the widest array of species.

Seeds

More than 20 different kinds of seeds are presently available on the market. Some are used in a pure form, while others are mixed to create a wider appeal. Studies have been done to see which seeds birds prefer and which one attracts the most species. The hands-down winner is black oil sunflower seed as the seed of choice for more species than any other. Low-priced mixes usually contain lower-quality seeds such as rape seed, oats, hulled wheat, and millets. Most birds will simply leave the seeds of these mixes in the feeder untouched. The following is a listing of some of the top seeds and what they attract.

BLACK OIL SUNFLOWER SEED
The champion of bird seeds. More species eat this seed than any other. More than 40 species are known to feed on this seed, from Cardinals to all the sparrows, Downy and Hairy Woodpeckers, and nuthatches.

STANDARD SUNFLOWER SEED
The second place in food choice. Cardinals, sparrows, goldfinch, House Finch, even mockingbirds are fond of this variety.

Note: seeds of the two sunflowers contain plant growth inhibitors that will keep grass and other plants from growing at the feeder site if the husks are left in a pile. Spring cleanup is a must. You can get shelled sunflower but remember that in wet weather they will swell up and mold easily, and this means you must clean the feeder on a more regular basis.

NIGER THISTLE
Imported from Africa and India, it is treated so it cannot germinate and compete with native plants. This is by far the preferred seed of goldfinches. Titmice also love these seeds, in addition to redpolls when they come in from the North. On the ground, Mourning Doves and juncos seem to enjoy them.

PEANUT HEARTS

These have taken on new importance in recent years. They are loved by titmice, Downy as well as other woodpeckers, Blue Jays, Eastern Towhees, mockingbirds, and even robins. Excellent for mixing in with suet when making seed blocks.

CRACKED CORN

Scattered on the ground or put in a feeding tray, this is the choice of turkey, pheasant, and bobwhite. Mourning Doves are also very fond of corn. Unfortunately, the blackbird group loves it too and can appear in massive flocks and dominate a feeding site.

SAFFLOWER SEED

A newcomer to the feeding scene that has gained attention as House Sparrows and starlings do not seem to eat it. Chickadees, nuthatches, jays, House Finches, White-throated Sparrows, and blackbirds, however, find it choice.

MILLETS (RED/BLACK/YELLOW)

Mainly a seed that cowbirds, House Sparrows, and grackles will feed on and that other birds will leave alone. Various species of sparrows and juncos will also eat millets, but they are not enough to compensate for the "pest" species it will attract. Low-priced bird-food mixes are composed mostly of these seeds.

BREAD

Bread and other baked goods, such as doughnuts, will be taken by birds, but in general they receive very few nutrients from breads. In addition, it's the less desirable species that tend to prefer bread products: House Sparrows, starlings, and grackles will stuff themselves with bread, and this, in turn, will keep them around the feeders where they can become a problem for less aggressive species.

SUET

Beef suet can be obtained from many markets and has proven to be the favorite of woodpeckers as well as nuthatches and chickadees. Titmice and Carolina Wrens will spend time at the suet feeder. If Pileated Woodpeckers are possible visitors, be sure the suet feeder is solidly anchored to a tree or post as hanging feeders will deter this large cautious woodpecker.

MEALWORMS

If you have bluebirds in your area you may want to consider placing mealworms (purchased from a pet store) in a shallow tray. I have seen old tuna cans placed on porch railings yield great results. Once the bluebirds find them, they will be constant visitors. One of my neighbors feeds at a regular time of day, and when he goes out to the feeder, the bluebirds land next to and even on him, taking mealworms from his fingers!

FRUIT

Many kinds of fruit can provide food for a wide variety of birds. Orioles love orange halves. Grapes, apples, even kiwis can provide a nutritious bounty. One oriole feeder in the Midwest has large bottle caps filled with grape jelly placed

A shallow can or dish anchored in the corner of a tray feeder (left) *is perfect for plac-ing out mealworms, which bluebirds relish. Orioles love to feed on orange halves* (right). *In this case the half is fixed to a special "pin" on a protected feeder.*

near the oriole feeders and the orioles can't get enough of the jelly! In the trop-ics, bananas and cooked rice are big favorites at feeding stations. One site has some 40 species arrive every morning to dine on this exotic combination. Birds constantly surprise us by how opportunistic they are. I was stunned in South America to watch as Caracaras came in to feed on spaghetti!

OME FRUITS TO TRY:

apples	robin (especially in winter), catbird, jays
oranges	orioles, woodpeckers
bananas	especially spring migrants (warblers, orioles, tanagers)
raisins	bluebirds, mockingbird, robin, tanagers
cooked rice	beloved in tropics by orioles, warblers, tanagers; people who have tried it in U.S. find it attracts many species
peanuts	blue jay
peanut butter and seed	chickadees, titmice, nuthatches, wintering warblers
grape jelly	orioles, catbird

VILD HARVEST

Acorns. In years of large mast (fruiting) crops of oaks, collect the acorns and store them until winter to provide an excellent food for species such as Red-headed Woodpeckers and Blue Jays. White Oak is the acorn of choice.

Melon Seeds. Dry out pumpkin, cantaloupe, and watermelon seeds and several species such as nuthatches, woodpeckers, chickadees, and titmice will enjoy them.

Cones. Collect pine and spruce cones just before they open to use as food for crossbills if they frequent your area. Opened cones can be used as hanging feeders. Smear peanut butter and seeds into the spread bracts, affix a wire or string, and hang in an area of feeding activity.

EGGSHELLS

When I went camping in the western mountains several years ago, a friend told me to crush up the eggshells after breakfast and spread them out. Sure enough, in a short time, Purple Martins were dropping down and feeding on them. I am sure other birds would also take advantage of this dietary supplement during the nesting period when calcium is in high demand. So if you have nesting martins nearby or just want to experiment, in the spring, try scattering finely crushed eggshells on the ground.

WATER

Water is an essential part of a complete bird-feeding station. Feather maintenance is very important to birds, and the bath not only provides drinking water but a place to clean the feathers. Commercial shallow bird baths tend to be the standard. Shallow depth is the key, and remember—when the birds are wet from a bath, their escape time is a bit delayed. Therefore, an escape distance of 10 feet (rather than 6 for the feeders) is recommended. In addition, dense cover such as an Arbor Vitae is recommended. The bird can quickly slip away from the site and dry off in the protection of dense cover.

The sound of water dripping or trickling is a great attraction for birds. In drought areas, be sure the water is recycled so that a large volume of water is not lost as it is splashed out or consumed. Add water and clean out the bird bath once a week to prevent algal growth. During the winter months heating units provide water even through the harshest weather.

Bird baths provide drinking and bathing water. Be sure they are shallow and that cover is available, as a wet bird is slightly slower in its escape response.

WHEN TO FEED BIRDS

Perhaps the most frequently asked questions about feeding birds concern *when* to feed them. When should I start feeding? When should I stop so I don't affect migration? Can I feed in the summer? Several issues must be considered.

People feed birds in order to enjoy them, so why not feed them all year long? As long as you're willing to put in the time to maintain the feeding area—supply food and water and keep the area clean—you will be rewarded by birds using the site. You may not get the variety in the summer that you'll see during migration or in the winter when there is more of a dependency on the feeder, but you may be rewarded with the antics of young birds being introduced to the site.

Birds can become dependent on feeders for supplemental food. It has been shown, however, that they do not rely on feeders for all of their food and perhaps not even a quarter of what they eat. That said, though, the feeder can be an important resource during times of duress. When severe snowstorms blanket wild food supplies, the birds will turn to the feeder they have come to know as a food resource. It is during these times of stress that the feeder plays its most vital role. *Do not let them down at this point!* If it is a storm of long duration, the feeding station may mean the difference of life for some of the more physiologically unprepared birds. The feeder helps many a bird through the hard times, so it is important to be faithful to your feeding once you start.

As for the question of affecting migration by holding the birds at the feeder so that they will not go north to breed or south for the winter, the answer is that birds are not controlled by food. Once the hormones for breeding begin to flow, they head north, and once the drive for migrating south takes hold, off they go, no matter how much food is available. If a species that normally does not stay for the summer or winter remains at the feeder, it is more than likely a young bird that does not have the proper hormonal impulse to migrate or an older bird that simply can no longer make extensive journeys. You are not affecting the breeding or migrant population of the birds of the United States by feeding.

PLANTINGS

You many want to enhance the feeding station area with plantings that can supplement what you feed. Remember, if you do decide to add plants to your feeder scheme, be sure you do not put them too close to the feeder, creating hiding areas for cats and other predators. It is best to use native plants. The birds are adapted to feeding on them already, and there is no chance of introduced plant species becoming invasive and causing problems with native plant populations. A few introduced plant species are listed here as they have proven to be excellent for birds and noninvasive. The following is not an exhaustive list by any means but will give you some ideas about enhancing your feeding area that you can expand on.

Plants for Attracting Specific Species

SUNFLOWER: goldfinches and other finches

These will grow large and need considerable space when the seed heads ripen and the plants begin to bend over. Harvest the mature seed heads and place them out on the feeder tray to provide an excellent food source, but be careful —the squirrels may dominate.

CHOKECHERRY: robins and mockingbirds

Small trees that are quite easy to grow and will provide a bountiful crop. The only drawback is the droppings of birds, which can stain cement, patios, and clothes hung out to dry.

MOUNTAIN ASH: Cedar and Bohemian Waxwings, robins

A beautiful small tree with clusters of deep orange berries. A wonderful food source that may attract the attention of several species, especially in the winter months. During invasion years by Pine Grosbeaks, these trees may host them for weeks.

COSMOS: goldfinches

Colorful and easy to grow, these nonnative plants are loved by goldfinches in the late summer.

TRUMPET CREEPER: hummingbirds

The large orange tubular flowers of this climbing vine are a favorite of Ruby-throated Hummingbirds. Care in maintaining the vines will keep them from overgrowing into ornamental trees.

IMPATIENS (TOUCH-ME-NOT): hummingbirds

Our native orange-flowered plants grow very well in wet areas and are a favorite food plant especially for hummingbirds in fall migration. The bright red cultivars can attract Ruby-throated Hummingbirds throughout the summer.

SCARLET BERGAMOT AND SALVIA: hummingbirds

These two cultivated plants are also hummingbird favorites. The bright red flowers will be visited constantly once they're discovered.

Widespread Attractants

Coniferous evergreens can play a threefold role in attracting birds. Some species of birds will use the dense foliage for night roosts. They often provide excellent cover, especially from attack by a predatory hawk. If old enough to produce cones, they can provide a food crop for winter finches, especially crossbills.

WHITE PINE: 48 species have been recorded feeding on the seeds in the cones, the needles, and even the resin!

YEWS: Excellent cover; some species feed on the seeds, which look like red berries.

REDCEDAR JUNIPER: A wide variety of species enjoy the small blue berrylike female cones. In one yard, 30 species were seen feeding on the cones in a one-month period in winter.

BLUEBERRY: Many species enjoy several native blueberries. Birds' love of blueberries is well documented by people who grow them for profit. If you want to simply add a supplemental food supply for fall migrants and residents in your feeder area, blueberries will do it.

SMOOTH AND STAGHORN SUMAC: Robins, as well as many other species, love sumac berries, especially in the winter. In the Northeast, where Common Flickers are becoming a regular wintering species, sumac berries are very popular. Because of the density of the fruiting head many insects find shelter there and species such as Downy Woodpeckers and Black-capped Chickadees will spend hours gleaning these insects from the fruiting bodies. Care must be used as sumacs can take over any open area and become a problem unless they're maintained.

WHITE OAKS: These very large handsome trees produce the sweet acorns favored by Blue Jays, Red-bellied and Red-headed Woodpeckers, and other species that store the acorns for winter.

Watching birds feed in the field will give added insight into what native species of plants can be attractive to you and your feeder visitors.

A Note on Shelter

If your yard is extensive and you provide nesting boxes during the summer, these boxes can be cleaned out after the nesting season, and several species may use the boxes as a night shelter. One friend had 10 Eastern Bluebirds that huddled in the same nesting box every night when the temperature plunged to the teens.

A properly constructed brush pile can also be a wonderful foraging, roosting, and escape site for birds. Make sure the limbs are stacked in alternate layers and not packed down. One caution: if there are a lot of cats in the area, you may not want a brush pile, as the cats will quickly learn to hide inside and capture entering birds.

THE SQUIRREL PROBLEM

Depending on what region of the country you live in and type of area(from urban to rural), in the eastern United States we have to contend with three species of squirrels. The widespread Gray Squirrel offers perhaps the greatest challenge and in many areas is the scourge of the feeder. Gray Squirrels are spread across the entire eastern portion of the United States. Fox Squirrels also cover a wide area but are missing from the Northeast and some of the Mid-Atlantic. Red Squirrels have an extensive range from Canada south to the northern portions of the Midwest, throughout the Northeast, and south through Ohio and Pennsylvania down the Appalachians as far as extreme northern Georgia. Therefore, if you feed, you will have some interaction with at least one species of squirrel, and in some areas, all three!

The Challenge of the Gray Squirrel

I believe that, if given time, the squirrels that inhabit my yard could become nuclear physicists! These animals are brilliant. They consistently solve the problem of how to get seeds from bird feeders, no matter what obstacles we may put in the way: elaborate flanges, weight-reaction levers, suspended feeders over water hazards, and on and on. The best we can hope for is to delay

Gray Squirrels represent the ultimate challenge at the feeding station. They are clever and persistent, and you will be taxed to your limit trying to keep these rascals from getting your seed.

17

them. Fortunately, there are enough new devices on the market that we can often make it through a feeding season without squirrel domination. The key seems to be in placing the feeder in an area that doesn't allow easy access.

There are many types of feeders available, all making numerous claims; choose carefully. Ask other birders what works for them. Ask the salesperson how well the feeder you're thinking of purchasing deters squirrels.

Remember that once you start to feed, no matter how well the antisquirrel feeder is touted, you will need to make modifications to fight the ongoing battle. Some people even enjoy the squirrels and let them feed or give them alternative food in the form of corn cobs on whirling arms or upright stakes. No matter how nicely you treat them and try to attract their attention elsewhere, they will eventually try to get to your seeds! So it's best to simply give in; enjoy feeding the birds and live in peaceful coexistence with the squirrels!

One caveat: do not try to capture squirrels and take them away. In some states or towns transport of any wild animal is illegal. In any case, there are more than enough squirrels to fill any opening you create. As fast as they are removed, more will move in to fill that opening. In most areas they have two broods of four to six young each year. One in the spring, the other in August. So repopulation is fairly easy even if only a couple pair are left in an area.

Fox Squirrels

Seemingly a little less persistent than Gray Squirrels, Fox Squirrels can nevertheless be a major problem. Follow the same advice as for Gray Squirrels.

Red Squirrels

These small, very active and attractive squirrels can do a lot of damage to a feeding site, as well as to nearby buildings. Normally found where there are evergreen trees, they soon develop a taste for what is available at the feeding tray. They can reach almost any feeder and will gnaw their way through plastic and wood to reach seeds or other foods. Very aggressive, they have been known to kill small songbirds, and if there is any nesting nearby, these little energy packets will find the nest and eat the eggs or even the young birds. They may even take up residence in the house, garage, or nearby shed. They can gnaw into the structure and destroy wiring, which can create a fire hazard. They are much more likely to attempt house entry than the Gray Squirrel is. The only defense is to attempt to thwart them with the same techniques you use for battling the Gray Squirrels.

PREDATORS

Predation by hawks and wild animals is a normal part of the life of birds. The greatest impact by far, however, is made by domestic cats. There are other predators that can also impact your feeder, some not quite as obvious as others. Red Squirrels will attack smaller birds and kill them. Common Grackles often act with "mob mentality." When a flock of grackles arrives at a feeder it is not uncommon to see a grackle attempt to kill smaller birds in order to steal the food in their crops. Whenever there is a concentration of birds there is a good chance that some form of predation will occur.

Cats

There are an estimated 70 million cats in the U.S., and a large number are feral. One study in Wisconsin estimated that rural cats killed some 19 million birds in that state alone in one year! When the country is considered on the whole, the number reaches astronomical proportions. Therefore, as mentioned in the section on feeders, it is important to place the feeder far enough away (6 feet) from any spot that could serve as cover for a cat. The only sure way to prevent cats from having an impact at the feeder is to see that cats are kept inside. You can ask your neighbors to keep their cats from entering your yard, explaining that you have gone to considerable efforts to create an active feeding station. Although belling a cat is often recommended (and studies have shown only multiple bells—not one—have an effect) it usually does not help a great deal in reducing attacks. Working with neighbors without antagonism may be the best approach.

In many areas, a natural control animal has moved in: the coyote. In some areas they will lower feral cat numbers fairly quickly.

Hawks

The birds of prey that consistently visit feeders to attack feeding birds is a group called the accipiters. Two species stand out: the Sharp-shinned Hawk and the Cooper's Hawk. The much larger Goshawk will also make attempts at large feeder birds, especially in northern areas. The first two are regularly seen near feeders. They may fly low to the ground to attempt to slip into an area unseen by the feeding birds. Ever-alert Blue Jays are their bane and are quick to call the alarm. Once the predator has been spotted, all the birds in the feeding area will chime in with their scolding chants and study it, watching its every move. Not until well after the hawk departs will they resume normal feeding. If the hawk slips in unnoticed, it will sit in a nearby bush totally still and with unending patience. When a feeding bird drops its guard, in it darts to pluck the bird from the site.

Cover and space are the best protection you can offer the feeding birds. The area around the feeder should be open enough for the birds to see the approach of a predator, yet close enough to cover for the birds to protect themselves from the hawk.

Owls

In northern areas where day-flying species such as Hawk Owls and Great Gray Owls live, these two species may attack birds at the feeder, especially if the food supply is limited. In other areas, since owls are nocturnal they do not have a great impact. Their greatest activity at feeder areas comes just before dawn when White-throated Sparrows, Dark-eyed Juncos, and cardinals give away their roosting positions. It is then that the owl can strike. Dense night-roost cover rather than open-limbed bushes can help to reduce predation.

Northern Shrikes

The "stealth" predator at the feeding station is the Northern Shrike. It doesn't look like a predator, and it may be unfamiliar to wintering birds whose territory it invades on irregular erruptions from the North. So it is an accepted part of the area, until its first attack, when it grabs a small bird from the feeder, and, lacking talons and incapable of killing the bird by force, it will often wedge the prey in the fork of a limb and peck or break the bird's neck with its large tooth-edged bill. After the attack, the feeder birds remember, and any appearance of the shrike will bring on screams and scolds as the birds head for cover. A place to run for cover is important, and although the shrike will chase birds through this cover the birds usually escape.

NIGHT VISITORS

A feeding station provides a tremendous amount of enjoyment during the day, but under the cover of darkness it can also attract creatures whose activities range from having no impact to being very destructive.

In suburban and rural settings, flying squirrels can become nightly visitors to the feeder. A common to abundant species, they go unseen by most as they move about late at night. Often the only indication of their visit is a pile of shelled seeds in a small mound where they sat and ate. They don't even leave tracks in the snow as they can glide from a tree up to 50 feet away and land perfectly on the feeding tray.

A few other nocturnal species can have a devastating effect. Husks, uneaten seeds, fruit remains, and other edibles are invitations to skunks, opossums, and raccoons. With their climbing ability, opossums and raccoons can reach most feeders and do not hesitate to rip into them to get at seed or other food. Skunks will stay on the ground and go for any scrap they can find. Be careful if you see any of these animals acting in a strange manner in the daytime as they may be rabid. A clean bird-feeding area is the best way to combat their noxious visits.

KEY TO RANGE MAPS

RED: summer range

BLUE: winter range

PURPLE: year-round range

RED DASH LINE: approximate limits of irregular summer range and/or post-breeding dispersal

BLUE DASH LINE: approximate limits of irregular winter range

PURPLE DASH LINE: approximate limits of irregular year-round range

HOW TO IDENTIFY BIRDS

Veteran birders will know how to use this book. Beginners, however, should spend some time becoming familiar in a general way with the illustrations. They are not arranged in systematic or phylogenetic order as in most orthological works but are grouped in 8 main visual categories:

(1) **Swimmers** — Ducks and ducklike birds
(2) **Aerialists** — Gulls and gull-like birds
(3) **Long-legged Waders** — Herons, cranes, etc.
(4) **Smaller Waders** — Plovers, sandpipers, etc.
(5) **Fowl-like Birds** — Grouse, quail, etc.
(6) **Birds of Prey** — Hawks, eagles, owls
(7) **Nonpasserine Land Birds**
(8) **Passerine (Perching) Birds**

Within these groupings it will be seen that ducks do not resemble loons; gulls are readily distinguishable from terns. The needlelike bills of warblers immediately differentiate them from the seed-cracking bills of sparrows. Birds that could be confused are grouped together when possible and are arranged in identical profile for direct comparison. The arrows point to outstanding "field marks" which are explained below.

WHAT IS THE BIRD'S SIZE?

Acquire the habit of comparing a new bird with some familiar "yardstick"—a House Sparrow, a robin, a pigeon, etc., so that you can say to yourself, "smaller than a robin; a little larger than a House Sparrow." The measurements in this book represent lengths in inches from bill tip to tail tip of specimens on their backs as in museum trays. However, specimen measurements vary widely depending on the preparator, who may have stretched the neck a bit.

The rewards of establishing a feeding station are many. An adult Red-headed Woodpecker is a dazzling visitor.

WHAT IS ITS SHAPE?

Is it plump like a Starling (left) or slender like a cuckoo (right)?

WHAT SHAPE ARE ITS WINGS?

Are they rounded like a Bobwhite's (left) or sharply pointed like a Barn Swallow's (right)?

WHAT SHAPE IS ITS BILL?

Is it small and fine like a warbler's (1); stout and short like a seed-cracking sparrow's (2); dagger-shaped like a tern's (3); or hook-tipped like that of a bird of prey (4)?

1   2   3   4

WHAT SHAPE IS ITS TAIL?

Is it deeply forked like a Barn Swallow's (1); square-tipped like a Cliff Swallow's (2); notched like a Tree Swallow's (3); rounded like a Blue Jay's (4); or pointed like a Mourning Dove's (5)?

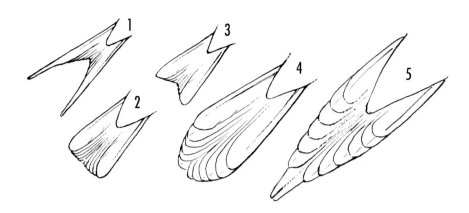

HOW DOES IT BEHAVE?

Does it cock its tail like a wren or hold it down like a flycatcher? Does it wag its tail? Does it sit erect on an open perch, dart after an insect, and return as a flycatcher does?

DOES IT CLIMB TREES?

If so, does it climb in spirals like a Creeper (left), in jerks like a woodpecker (center) using its tail as a brace, or does it go down headfirst like a nuthatch (right)?

25

HOW DOES IT FLY?

Does it undulate (dip up and down) like a Flicker (1)? Does it fly straight and fast like a Dove (2)? Does it hover like a Kingfisher (3)? Does it glide or soar?

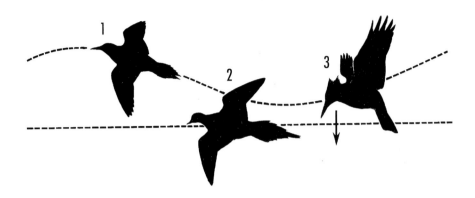

DOES IT SWIM?

Does it sit low in the water like a loon (1) or high like a gallinule (2)? If a duck, does it dive like a deepwater duck (3); or does it dabble and upend like a Mallard (4)?

DOES IT WADE?

Is it large and long-legged like a heron or small like a sandpiper? If one of the latter, does it probe the mud or pick at things? Does it teeter or bob?

WHAT ARE ITS FIELD MARKS?

Some birds can be identified by color alone, but most birds are not that easy. The most important aids are what we call field marks, which are, in effect, the "trademarks of nature." Note whether the breast is spotted as in the Wood Thrush (1); streaked as in the thrasher (2); or plain as in a cuckoo (3).

TAIL PATTERNS

Does the tail have a "flash pattern"—a white tip as in the Kingbird (1); white patches in the outer corners as in the towhee (2); or white sides as in the junco (3)?

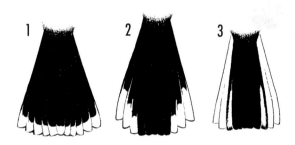

RUMP PATCHES

Does it have a light rump like a Cliff Swallow (1) or flicker (2)? The harrier, Yellow-rumped "Myrtle" Warbler, and many of the shorebirds also have distinctive rump patches.

27

EYE-STRIPES AND EYE-RINGS

Does the bird have a stripe above, through, or below the eye, or a combination of these stripes? Does it have a striped crown? A ring around the eye or "spectacles"? A "mustache" stripe? These details are important in many small songbirds.

WINGBARS

Do the wings have light wingbars or not? Their presence or absence is important in recognizing many warblers, vireos, and flycatchers. Wingbars may be single or double, bold or obscure.

WING PATTERNS

The basic wing patterns of ducks (shown below), shorebirds, and other water birds are very important. Notice whether the wings have patches (1) or stripes (2); are solidly colored (3) or have contrasting black tips (Snow Goose, etc.).

TOPOGRAPHY OF A BIRD

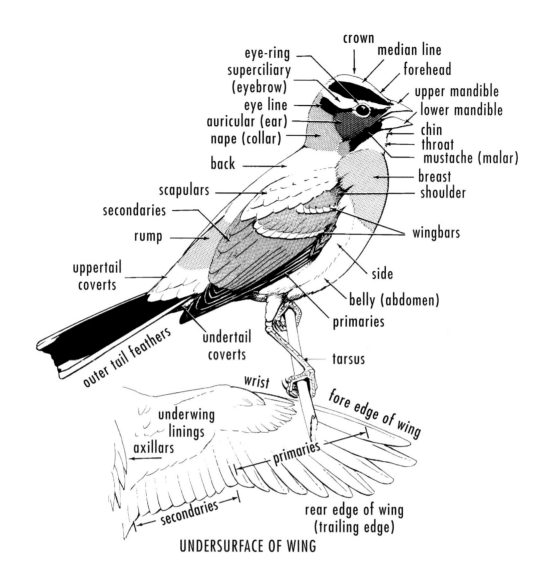

UNDERSURFACE OF WING

OTHER TERMS USED IN THIS BOOK

GENDER SYMBOLS: ♂ means male, ♀ means female. These symbols are used frequently on the plates, sparingly in the text.

ACCIDENTAL: In the area of this book, recorded fewer than 15 times; far out of range. On the state level only 1 or 2 records; might not be expected again.

CASUAL: Very few records, but might be expected again.

INTRODUCED: Not native; deliberately released.

EXOTIC: Not native; either released or escaped.

IN PART: A well-marked subspecies or form—part of a species.

QUICK REFERENCE FOOD LIST

These are the preferred foods of some common feeder birds.

Oil sunflower = black oil sunflower seeds
Peanut butter mix = peanut butter with various seeds mixed in
Suet cakes = melted suet, seeds, raisins, chopped peanuts

SPECIES	FOOD
Blackbird, Red-winged	cracked corn, shelled sunflower seed
Bluebird, Eastern	mealworms, raisins
Bobwhite, Northern	cracked corn, corn
Bunting, Indigo	Niger thistle, proso millet
Cardinal, Northern	oil sunflower, peanut hearts
Catbird, Gray	fruiting shrubs, apples, mealworms, grape jelly
Chickadee, Black-capped	oil sunflower, suet, peanut hearts
Chickadee, Boreal	oil sunflower, peanut hearts, pumpkin seeds, suet
Cowbird, Brown-headed	deter from feeder by using safflower
Creeper, Brown	peanut butter mix, suet cakes
Crossbills, Red/White-winged	conifer cone seeds, sunflower
Crow, American	cracked corn, scraps, anything available
Dove, Mourning	sunflower, sorghum, millet and grass seeds
Finch, House	oil sunflower, cracked corn, peanut hearts, millet
Finch, Purple	peanut hearts, pumpkin seeds, sunflower, safflower
Flicker, Northern	suet, peanut hearts, raisins, apples
Goldfinch, American	Niger thistle, sunflower pieces
Grackle, Common	sunflower seeds, cracked corn, fruit
Grosbeak, Evening	oil sunflower, safflower seeds, peanut bits
Grosbeak, Pine	oil sunflower, highbush cranberry, ash samaras
Grosbeak, Rose-breasted	oil sunflower, fruit
Hummingbird, Ruby-throated	sugar water in feeders
Hummingbird, Rufous	sugar water in feeders
Jay, Blue	oil sunflower, peanuts, acorns, fruit
Jay, Gray	suet, suet mix, scraps
Junco, Dark-eyed	sunflower, millet, peanut hearts

Kinglet, Ruby-crowned/Golden-crowned	peanut hearts, fruit
Magpie, Black-billed	almost anything (seeds to meat scraps)
Martin, Purple	crushed eggshells to enhance diet in spring
Mockingbird, Northern	apples, raisins, mealworms, rose hips
Nuthatch, Red-breasted	suet, oil sunflower, peanut butter mix
Nuthatch, White-breasted	suet, peanuts, oil sunflower, safflower
Oriole, Baltimore	orange halves, apples, grape jelly, mealworms
Oriole, Bullock's	orange halves, sunflower, mealworms, apples
Pheasant, Ring-necked	cracked corn, corn
Raven, Common	cracked corn, meat scraps
Redpoll, Common	Niger thistle, peanut hearts, oil sunflower
Robin, American	apples, raisins, sumac, mountain ash, chokecherry
Sapsucker, Yellow-bellied	apple slices, suet, sugar water
Siskin, Pine	Niger thistle, hulled sunflower
Sparrow, American Tree	millet, oil sunflower
Sparrow, Chipping	red and white millet, mealworms
Sparrow, Fox	cracked corn, peanut hearts, sunflower seeds
Sparrow, House	almost anything — dislikes safflower seeds
Sparrow, Lark	oil sunflower
Sparrow, Song	red and white millet, oil sunflower, peanut hearts
Sparrow, White-crowned	millet and grass seeds, sunflower
Starling, European	eats everything — dislikes safflower seeds
Tanager, Scarlet	orange halves, sunflower, suet, peanut hearts
Tanager, Summer	sunflower seeds, suet, raisins
Thrasher, Brown	sunflower, fruit, dogwood, redcedar juniper
Thrush, Varied	sunflower, berries, redcedar juniper
Titmouse, Tufted	oil sunflower, suet, peanut hearts, safflower, fruit
Towhee, Eastern	cracked corn, sunflower, pumpkin seeds
Turkey, Wild	cracked corn, corn
Warbler, Orange-crowned	orange slices, suet, peanut butter mix
Warbler, Yellow-rumped	orange slices, peanut butter mix, suet
Woodpecker, Downy	suet, suet cakes, peanut butter mix
Woodpecker, Hairy	suet, oil sunflower, will take nectar
Woodpecker, Pileated	suet, will take oil sunflower
Woodpecker, Red-bellied	cracked corn, suet, orange, peanuts
Woodpecker, Red-headed	acorns, suet, peanut butter mix

TITMICE Family Paridae

Small, plump birds. Often acrobatic while feeding. Very often travel in groups in mixed-species flocks with kinglets and warblers. FOOD IN WILD: Insects, seeds, berries.

BLACK-CAPPED CHICKADEE
Poecile atricapillus   **to 5½"**

VOICE: A distinct *chic-a-dee-dee-dee*. Song is a clear, whistled *fee-bee*, with the first note higher.

FOOD: Oil sunflower seed, peanut butter and seed mix, suet.

NOTES: These trusting birds often forage in flocks. In fall and winter they often mix with other woodland species. Periodic winter influxes southward.

CAROLINA CHICKADEE
Poecile carolinensis   **4½"**

VOICE: A high, rapid *tish-ta-dee-dee*, delivered faster than the notes of the Black-capped. Call is 4-parted *fee-bee-fee-bay*.

FOOD: Same as Black-capped.

NOTES: Has a small bib; less white in wing. Hybrids have occurred.

BOREAL CHICKADEE
Poecile hudsonicus   **to 5½"**

VOICE: A slow, drawn out, raspy *chick-che-day-day*.

FOOD: In North will feed on meat of hung deer or moose rib cages. Suet and sunflower seeds in hanging feeders.

NOTES: Often tame, the Boreal has a brown cap and extensive pinkish brown sides. Sporadically wanders south in winter.

TUFTED TITMOUSE *Baeolophus bicolor*   **6"**

VOICE: A clearly whistled *peter-peter-peter* or *here-here-here*. Also delivers a variety of whistles and wheezy plaintive notes.

FOOD: Oil sunflower seed, peanut butter and seed mix. Suet. Will carry food away to cache.

NOTES: A stalwart at the bird feeder, the Tufted Titmouse has a perky crest and black button eyes. Its population is expanding in many areas.

BLACK-CAPPED
CHICKADEE

CAROLINA
CHICKADEE

BOREAL
CHICKADEE

immature

adult

TUFTED
TITMOUSE

NUTHATCHES Family Sittidae

Small, stout tree hunters with strong bills, nuthatches often climb headfirst down tree trunks or forage upside down on limbs. FOOD IN WILD: Insect eggs, seeds, nuts.

WHITE-BREASTED NUTHATCH
Sitta carolinensis   **to 6"**
VOICE: A series of rapid low, nasal *yank-yank-yanks*.
FOOD: Sunflower seeds and peanut hearts in hanging feeders. Suet blocks.
NOTES: Male has a black cap. Inquisitive.

RED-BREASTED NUTHATCH
Sitta canadensis   **to 4½"**
VOICE: A high, fast, repeated *ank-ank-ank*.
FOOD: Hanging suet blocks. Oil sunflower seeds, peanut hearts.
NOTES: Explores tree limbs more than trunks. Flits wings when excited.

BROWN-HEADED NUTHATCH
Sitta pusilla   **to 4½"**
VOICE: A high rapid *kit-kit-kit* and a piping *ki-day-ki-day*. Groups twitter and chatter.
FOOD: Suet may work. Peanut hearts in hanging feeders. Oil sunflower seed.
NOTES: Often heard from high in pines before seen.

CREEPERS Family Certhiidae

Creepers are small, slim, and stiff-tailed. Their plumage allows them to blend well with tree bark. Curved bill aids in probing. FOOD IN WILD: Insect eggs, insects.

BROWN CREEPER *Certhia americana*   **5"**
VOICE: A single, high *see*. Song is a twittering jumble of musical notes.
FOOD: Suet. Prefers to creep up tree to underside.
NOTES: Forages by creeping up trees and then dropping to base of next tree and spiraling up. Hides nest behind loose flap of bark. Scattered nesting records south of mapped range.

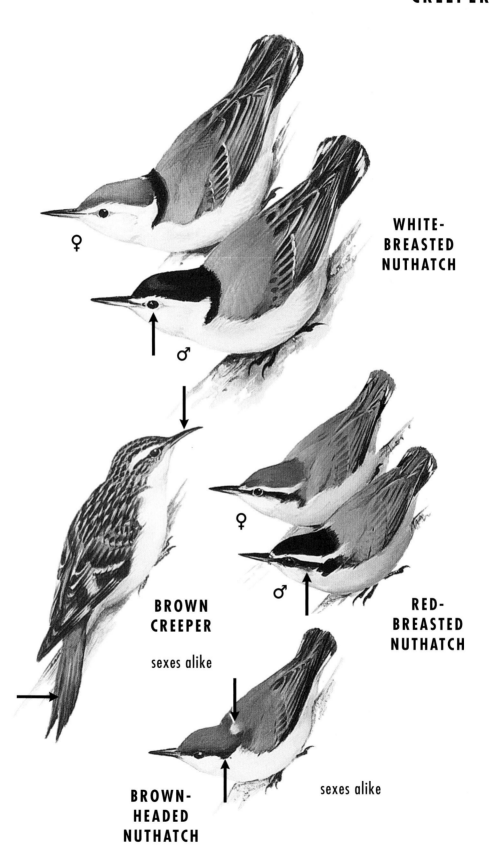

♀

♂

WHITE-
BREASTED
NUTHATCH

♀

♂

RED-
BREASTED
NUTHATCH

BROWN
CREEPER

sexes alike

BROWN-
HEADED
NUTHATCH

sexes alike

WOODPECKERS Family Picidae

Woodpeckers are chisel-billed, wood-boring birds. Their feet and stiff tail feathers are designed to anchor them in place on tree trunks. They all excavate holes to nest in. Flight is undulating. Most males have red on head. **FOOD IN WILD:** Tree-boring insects, berries, acorns, tree sap.

DOWNY WOODPECKER
Picoides pubescens   **to 6½"**

VOICE: A rapid whinny of descending notes. Also a sharp *pick* (Hairy's is a *peek*).

FOOD: One of the most common feeder birds. Loves suet and oil sunflower seed.

NOTES: Male has a solid red patch on back of head. Common birdfeeder species.

HAIRY WOODPECKER
Picoides villosus   **to 9½"**

VOICE: A fast, dry rattle. Note is a sharp *peek*.

FOOD: Suet, peanut hearts, sunflower seed, mealworms, and fruit.

NOTES: A midsized woodpecker with a larger bill than the Downy. Male's red patch has a black line through it. Outer tail feathers are pure white. Numbers are dropping in many areas in the East.

THREE-TOED WOODPECKER
Picoides tridactylus   **to 9½"**

VOICE: A sharp *kick* or *tick*.

FOOD: If it shows up at feeder, will take suet, sunflower seed, mealworms.

NOTES: Yellow cap and only 3 toes. Chips bark scales from trees rather than digging holes. Rare wanderer south to dash line.

BLACK-BACKED WOODPECKER
Picoides arcticus   **to 10"**

VOICE: A sharp *chuck*.

FOOD: See Three-toed.

NOTES: Has a yellow cap (male), 3 toes, and a black back. Rare at feeders.

WOODPECKERS

DOWNY WOODPECKER

HAIRY WOODPECKER

♂ southern form

THREE-TOED WOODPECKER

BLACK-BACKED WOODPECKER

NORTHERN (Yellow-shafted) FLICKER

Colaptes auratus (in part)   **to 14"**

VOICE: A rolling *wick, ka wick, ka wick, ka wick* or squeaky *flick-a, flick-a*.

FOOD: Takes suet, peanuts, mealworms.

NOTES: A large woodpecker with distinct white rump that flashes when it takes off. Yellow shafting to wing feathers. Male has a black mustache. Fond of ants, so often flushes from ground.

NORTHERN (Red-shafted) FLICKER

Colaptes auratus (in part)

Western color variant. Note salmon shafting to wing feathers. Male has a red mustache. Ranges of these 2 color variants overlap on Great Plains. Very rare in East.

FOOD: See Yellow-shafted.

RED-BELLIED WOODPECKER

Melanerpes carolinus   **to 10½"**

VOICE: A nasal *chiv-chiv* or *churr-churr*.

FOOD: Oranges, acorns, suet, sunflower seeds.

NOTES: Laddered back with great deal of red on head. Red on belly is difficult to see. Expanding its range northward.

RED-COCKADED WOODPECKER

Picoides borealis   **to 8½"**

VOICE: A rough, rasping *sripp* or *zhilp*.

FOOD: Does not come to feeders.

NOTES: Endangered. Back is zebra-striped; small spot of red on male's head. Very local resident within range.

YELLOW-BELLIED SAPSUCKER

Sphyrapicus varius   **to 9"**

VOICE: A nasal mewing. Drumming—several rapid taps—followed by slow series.

FOOD: Apples, suet, sugar water.

NOTES: Large white wing patches and white rump. Drills orderly rows of small holes, often covering trunk of tree, for sap and to attract insect prey.

WOODPECKERS

Yellow-shafted form

Red-shafted form

♂

Red-shafted

Yellow-shafted

♂

♀

NORTHERN FLICKER
Yellow-shafted form

immature

♀

♂

RED-BELLIED WOODPECKER

♂

RED-COCKADED WOODPECKER

immature

♂

YELLOW-BELLIED SAPSUCKER

39

RED-HEADED WOODPECKER

Melanerpes erythrocephalus   **to 9½"**

VOICE: A loud *queer* or *queeah.*

FOOD: Acorns, oranges, sunflower seeds, peanut chunks.

NOTES: The only woodpecker in the East with an all-red head. Has large white wing patches and a white rump. Will establish winter territories defending stored acorns.

PILEATED WOODPECKER

Dryocopus pileatus   **to 19½"**

VOICE: A loud, echoing *kik-kik-kikik-kikkik.* Hammering in deep, well-spaced thuds.

FOOD: Will take suet and suet cakes if anchored to tree, not hanging. Sunflower seeds.

NOTES: A crow-sized woodpecker with a flaming red crest and a white-striped face. Makes holes that are large rectangles. Southern birds are tamer than those in the North.

IVORY-BILLED WOODPECKER

Campephilus principalis   **to 20"**

VOICE: A loud tooting.

NOTES: Believed to be extinct; there have been no confirmed sightings since the 1950s. Habitat preference was the river bottom country of S.C. to Florida west to eastern Texas.

WOODPECKERS

immature

adult

RED-HEADED WOODPECKER
sexes similar

♂

♀

under

PILEATED WOODPECKER

♀

under

♂

upper

IVORY-BILLED WOODPECKER
extinct

41

GROSBEAKS, FINCHES, SPARROWS, BUNTINGS
Families Fringillidae, Emberizidae, Cardinalidae

Seed-cracking bills range from massive in grosbeaks to conical in sparrows to cross-tipped in crossbills. **FOOD IN WILD:** Seeds, fruit, insects.

NORTHERN CARDINAL
Cardinalis cardinalis   to 9"
VOICE: A clear, whistled *what-cheer, what-cheer* followed by *whoit, whoit, whoit.* Call note is a sharp, metallic *chip.*
FOOD: Oil sunflower seed is its favorite. Peanut hearts. Spread seed over wide area to attract more individuals.
NOTES: One of the best known birds because of its color. Expanding its range north. A common visitor to feeders.

RED CROSSBILL *Loxia curvirostra*   to 6½"
VOICE: A finchlike warble: *jip, jip, jip, jeeaa, jeeaa.* Call note is a *jip-jip* or *kip-kip.*
FOOD: When it comes to feeders, oil sunflower seed is its choice. Also will take seeds from harvested cones.
NOTES: Bill is unique to crossbills; it is used to open evergreen cones. Flocks visiting from North are often tame. Dangles from cones as it feeds.

WHITE-WINGED CROSSBILL
Loxia leucoptera   to 6⁷⁄₁₀"
VOICE: A succession of loud trills at different pitches. Call note is a liquid *peet* or dry *chif-chif.*
FOOD: Same as for Red Crossbill. Less common at feeders than Red Crossbill.
NOTES: Particularly fond of hemlocks. Very rarely visits feeders.

RED FINCHES

juvenile

♂

♀

NORTHERN
CARDINAL

♀

♂

immature

RED
CROSSBILL

♂

♀

WHITE-WINGED
CROSSBILL

EVENING GROSBEAK
Coccothraustes vespertinus   8"

VOICE: A finchlike warble. Also ringing finchlike calls: *cleer-cleer* or *cleer-ip*.

FOOD: Oil sunflower seed is its favorite; they will spend days emptying feeders.

NOTES: An exotic-looking bird. Often works feeders through a winter. Irregular; major movements some years south to dash line.

AMERICAN GOLDFINCH   *Carduelis tristis*   5"

VOICE: Sustained, clear, and canary-like. Flight call: *per-chick-o-ree*.

FOOD: Niger thistle seeds from special hanging feeders or hanging bags.

NOTES: Dramatic plumage change from summer to winter. Eats thistle seeds at feeder.

PINE SISKIN   *Carduelis pinus*   to 5"

VOICE: A goldfinchlike song. Call notes are a loud *chleee-ip* or a high upward-slurred *shreeeee*.

FOOD: Niger thistle seeds and sunflower seeds. Will also take suet cake mix.

NOTES: Sporadic in its movements from more northern areas. Following invasion years, may breed south to dash line.

EUROPEAN GOLDFINCH
Carduelis carduelis   5½"

This Eurasian introduction established itself for a short while on Long Island. The colony is now extirpated. Escaped birds occasionally appear at feeders to feed on thistle and sunflower seed.

♀

♂

**EVENING
GROSBEAK**

♂ winter

♂ summer

♀

**AMERICAN
GOLDFINCH**

♂

♀

PINE SISKIN

sexes similar

EUROPEAN GOLDFINCH

45

COMMON REDPOLL *Carduelis flammea*   5"

VOICE: A trill followed by a rattling *chet-chet-chet*. Flight call: a rattling *chet-chet-chet-chet*.

FOOD: Loves to visit hanging feeders for sunflower seeds, Niger thistle.

NOTES: An erratic winter invader from the North to dash line. Often visits feeders with goldfinch flocks.

HOARY REDPOLL *Carduelis hornemanni*   5"

VOICE: Calls and song like Common Redpoll's.

FOOD: Same as for Common Redpoll.

NOTES: A frosty white bird. Bill is smaller than Common Redpoll's. Much rarer wanderer to northern states south to dash line.

HOUSE FINCH

Carpodacus mexicanus   **to 5⁷/₁₀"**

VOICE: A bright, loose, disjointed series of sweet notes that often ends with *wheer*.

FOOD: Dominant at feeders. Flocks will spend whole day emptying sunflower seeds, peanut hearts, cracked corn.

NOTES: A western species introduced to the East in 1940s. Colonization of U.S. is nearly complete. Flocks often take over bird feeders.

PURPLE FINCH

Carpodacus purpureus   **to 6"**

VOICE: A fast, lively warbler with jumbled sweet notes. Flight note: *pik*.

FOOD: Oil sunflower seed, pumpkin seeds.

NOTES: Appears to have been ousted from feeders by invading House Finches.

PINE GROSBEAK *Pinicola enucleator* **to 10"**

VOICE: A whistled *tee-tew-tew* like that of a yellowlegs but low-pitched.

FOOD: Sunflower seeds. Loves highbush cranberry fruits and crabapple.

NOTES: A sporadic winter visitor south to dash line. Often very tame.

RED FINCHES, etc.

♀

♂

orange
variant

♀

♂

HOUSE
FINCH

COMMON
REDPOLL

HOARY
REDPOLL

♂

♀

♂

PURPLE
FINCH

immature ♂

♀

♂

PINE GROSBEAK

DARK-EYED ("Slate-colored") JUNCO
Junco hyemalis **to 6½"**
VOICE: A loose, musical trill like that of a Pine Warbler or Chipping Sparrow, but smoother.
FOOD: Oil sunflower seed, millet, cracked corn. A common visitor to the winter feeder.

DARK-EYED ("Oregon") JUNCO
Junco hyemalis **to 6½"**
VOICE: Similar to that of the "Slate-colored."
NOTES: A western form that turns up at feeding stations in the East. Their white outer tail feather as they fly up from the roadside in the winter is a common sight.

SNOW BUNTING
Plectrophenax nivalis **to 7⅕"**
VOICE: A musical *ti-ti-chu-ree*. Call note is a sharp whistled *teer* or *tew*, also a rolling *brrreeet*.
FOOD: Although mainly birds of open field and shoreline in the winter, they do come to feeders on occasion. They forage on the ground, taking millet, cracked corn, and oil sunflower seed.
NOTES: No other songbird shows so much white, but beware of albino or leucistic individuals of other species. Often overlooked, as it blends in with snow and grasses.

"SNOWBIRDS"

DARK-EYED
("Slate-colored")
JUNCO

♀

juvenile

♂

DARK-EYED
("Oregon")
JUNCO

♂

♀

♀ winter

♂ winter

♂ summer

SNOW
BUNTING

49

JAYS Family Corvidae

Large- to medium-sized birds. Their strong bills are covered with bristles at the base. Sexes look alike. **FOOD IN WILD:** Nearly anything edible.

BLUE JAY *Cyanocitta cristata* to 12½"
VOICE: A harsh, slurred *jay*, a musical *queedle*.
FOOD: Favorite food is acorns. Oil sunflower seed, fruits, peanuts.
NOTES: Large, colorful, and well known, the Blue Jay moves in large groups in the fall. Mimics hawk calls and loves to feed on acorns it stores for winter.

FLORIDA SCRUB-JAY
Aphelocoma coerulescens to 12"
VOICE: A rasping *kwesh-kwesh*, also *zhrink*.
FOOD: Not typical at feeders. Oranges, sunflower seeds. Omnivorous.
NOTES: Has now been separated as a full species from 2 other western species.

GRAY JAY
Perisoreus canadensis to 13"
VOICE: A soft *whee-ah*. Also makes gurgled notes and even chatters harshly.
FOOD: Often very tame. Visits camps for handouts. Will feed on deer or moose rib cages. Suet, Peanut butter and seed mix.
NOTES: Looks like a huge chickadee!

BLACK-BILLED MAGPIE *Pica pica*
to 22" (including long green tail)
VOICE: A harsh, rapid *queg, queg, queg, queg,* or nasal *maaag* or *aag-aaag*.
FOOD: Omnivorous. If it does come to a feeder, will take seeds, fruit, suet.
NOTES: Rare to the East, the Black-billed Magpie makes a huge ball-like nest of sticks.

JAYS,
MAGPIES

sexes alike

BLUE JAY

FLORIDA
SCRUB-JAY

GRAY JAY

adult

GRAY JAY
juvenile

BLACK-BILLED
MAGPIE

51

MOCKINGBIRDS and THRASHERS Family Mimidae

Excellent songsters. Mockingbird mimics other species and may sing at night. **FOOD IN WILD:** Fruits and insects.

BROWN THRASHER *Toxostoma rufum* 11½"
VOICE: A succession of clear notes and raspy phrases sung in couplets.
FOOD: Not common at feeders. Corn, peanuts, sunflower seeds, raisins, suet on ground.
NOTES: Runs on ground in pursuit of insects.

GRAY CATBIRD *Dumetella carolinensis* 9"
VOICE: Catlike mewing, grating *check-check*. Song is a series of disjunct phrases and notes.
FOOD: Not a common feeder bird. Fruiting shrubs (blueberry, chokecherry). Mealworms, apples, grape jelly.
NOTES: Abundant thicket species. Flicks tail as it peers from thickets.

NORTHERN MOCKINGBIRD
Mimus polyglottos **to 11"**
VOICE: A jumbled series of notes and phrases, often mimicking other species. Unmated males sing through the night.
FOOD: Attracted to plantings, especially rose hips and berries. Fruit, raisins, suet.
NOTES: Has spread north, rarely and irregularly to dash line.

THRUSHES Family Turdidae

TOWNSEND'S SOLITAIRE *Myadestes townsendi* 8"
A rare visitor from the West and placed here for comparison to Mockingbird. Distinguished by its eye-ring and buff wing patches. Winter has been the best time for recording this western straggler. Not a feeder bird but could occur in plantings such as Redcedar Juniper.

MOCKINGBIRDS, THRASHERS

sexes alike

BROWN THRASHER

GRAY CATBIRD

NORTHERN MOCKINGBIRD

flight pattern

wing flashing

shrike for comparison

TOWNSEND'S SOLITAIRE
(a thrush)

53

WRENS Family Troglodytidae

Small, energetic, furtive brown birds. Slightly curved bill; tail is held cocked up. **FOOD IN WILD:** Insects and spiders. Will take suet at feeders.

HOUSE WREN *Troglodytes aedon*   to 5"
VOICE: A stuttering musical song that rises in the middle and falls at the end.
FOOD: Suet, peanut hearts, hulled sunflower seed.
NOTES: Can dominate all bird boxes in a yard.

WINTER WREN *Troglodytes troglodytes*   4"
VOICE: A beautiful long series of tinkling notes.
FOOD: Slips in to feed on suet, peanut hearts, shelled sunflower seed, fruit.
NOTES: Tiny skulker of shadowed areas.

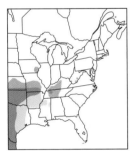

BEWICK'S WREN
Thryomanes bewickii   to 5⅕"
VOICE: A series of notes dropping slightly at the end.
FOOD: Will take suet, oil sunflower seed, mealworms, fruit.
NOTES: White edge to tail. Overall decline.

CAROLINA WREN
Thryothorus ludovicianus   5⁷⁄₁₀"
VOICE: A clear *tea-kettle, tea-kettle, tea-kettle.*
FOOD: Loves to live in brush piles and tangles. At tray or hanging feeder will eat suet, hulled sunflower seed, oil sunflower seed, and fruits.
NOTES: Populations are reduced by severe winters. Sporadic north to dash line.

HOUSE WREN

WINTER WREN

BEWICK'S WREN

CAROLINA WREN

55

BLACKBIRDS, ORIOLES, etc. Family Icteridae

A varied group possessing conical, sharp-pointed bills and rather flat profiles. Some are black and iridescent; others are highly colored. **FOOD IN WILD:** Insects, small fruits, seeds, waste grain.

RED-WINGED BLACKBIRD
Agelaius phoeniceus **to 9½"**

VOICE: Call note is a loud *check* and high, slurred whistle: *terrr-eeee*. Song is a liquid *o-ka-lee*.

FOOD: Cracked corn, shelled sunflower seed. Flocks can dominate feeders.

NOTES: Very gregarious. The voice of the spring marsh. Male's brilliant epaulets flare in display.

YELLOW-HEADED BLACKBIRD
Xanthocephalus xanthocephalus **to 11"**

VOICE: An electronic buzzing with interspersed croaks, whistles, and rasping notes.

FOOD: Ground feeder. Grains, small seeds, cracked corn.

NOTES: A prairie species that occasionally appears in grackle and blackbird flocks east to the East Coast, typically in the fall and winter.

BROWN-HEADED COWBIRD
Molothrus ater **to 7"**

VOICE: Flight call is a *weeee-titi*. Song is a gurgling, bubbling, upward *glug glug gleee*.

FOOD: An undesirable at the feeder. Favorites of cracked corn and millet should not be placed out. Effect on songbird population is extreme.

NOTES: Brown-headed Cowbirds have had a distinct impact on some species, as they are nest parasites, leaving eggs in other birds' nests. The more edge created, the more woodland birds are affected. Note high cock to tail when feeding in mixed blackbird flocks.

ICTERIDS
(BLACKBIRDS, etc.)

epaulets
concealed

immature ♂

epaulets in
display

♀

♂

♂

RED-WINGED BLACKBIRD

♀

YELLOW-HEADED
BLACKBIRD

♂

♀

♂

BROWN-HEADED
COWBIRD

juvenile

immature ♂ molting

57

RUSTY BLACKBIRD *Euphagus carolinus* 9"

VOICE: Call note is a sharp *chack*. Song is a split creak like a rusty hinge: *kush-a-lee*.

FOOD: Occasionally will stop in migration. Will take hulled sunflower seed and cracked corn.

NOTES: Male attains rusty marks only in the fall. Forages for food on ground, flipping wet leaves.

BREWER'S BLACKBIRD

Euphagus cyanocephalus **to 9"**

VOICE: A harsh, wheezy, creaking *queee-ee*.

FOOD: When this species has shown up at eastern feeders it has taken cracked corn, hulled sunflower seed, and oranges.

NOTES: A scarce visitor to the East Coast.

COMMON GRACKLE

Quiscalus quiscula **to 13½"**

VOICE: Split rasping notes with calls of *chack*.

FOOD: Not to be attracted. Can disrupt feeders and even kill smaller birds. Dislikes safflower seeds.

NOTES: Gregarious; forages in huge flocks. The two color races, "purple" and "bronze," were considered separate species at one time.

BOAT-TAILED GRACKLE

Quiscalus major **to 16½"**

VOICE: A jumble of harsh clicks, buzzes, and whistles. Large roosting flocks can be deafening.

FOOD: See Common Grackle.

NOTES: Extending range north. Overlaps with Great-tailed Grackle in coastal Texas and Louisiana.

GREAT-TAILED GRACKLE

Quiscalus mexicanus **to 18"**

VOICE: Buzzes, clicks, and cackles like the Boat-tailed. Also sounds a harsh *check check*.

FOOD: See Common Grackle.

NOTES: Male has flatter head and larger tail than male Boat-tailed Grackle. Extending range north.

ICTERIDS
(BLACKBIRDS, etc.)

♂ summer

♀

♂ winter

RUSTY
BLACKBIRD

BREWER'S
BLACKBIRD

♀

♂ winter   ♂ summer

♂

♂

purple race

Atlantic
Coast

♀

bronze
race

COMMON
GRACKLE

♀

♂

♂

Gulf
states

GREAT-
TAILED
GRACKLE

♀

BOAT-TAILED
GRACKLE

ROSE-BREASTED GROSBEAK
Pheucticus ludovicianus　　　　**to 8½"**

VOICE: A smooth rising and falling of mellow notes. Call note is a metallic *eek*.

FOOD: Seen at feeders mainly during migration. Oil sunflower seed. Loves cherry blossoms.

NOTES: Rare at winter feeders. May hybridize with the Black-headed.

BLACK-HEADED GROSBEAK
Pheucticus melanocephalus　　　　**to 7⁷⁄₁₀"**

VOICE: Voice is like that of the Rose-breasted.

FOOD: Mixed seeds, oil sunflower seed.

NOTES: Appears at feeders. Female has a yellow or buff chest with little streaking compared to the female Rose-breasted.

GREEN-TAILED TOWHEE
Pipilo chlorurus　　　　**6½"**

Another stray to the East from the West. Usually recorded at winter feeders. Has a white chin and a rich, rusty cap. Will take sunflower seed and millet.

EASTERN TOWHEE
Pipilo erythrophthalmus　　　　**to 8½"**

VOICE: A distinct *drink-your-teeeee*, with the last syllable higher. Also a loud *chewink* with a rising inflection.

FOOD: Feeds mainly on the ground, at times on deck or tray. Uses both feet to "double scratch." Sunflower seeds, cracked corn, pumpkin seeds.

NOTES: White-eyed race in South. Uses both feet to double-scratch in leaves.

SPOTTED TOWHEE
Pipilo maculata　　　　**to 8½"**

VOICE: Call a slurred, whiny, scratchy *twee*.

HABITAT: Brushy areas.

NOTES: Occurs east to plains states.

GROSBEAKS, TOWHEES

ROSE-BREASTED GROSBEAK

♂

♀

BLACK-HEADED GROSBEAK

♀

♂

GREEN-TAILED TOWHEE

♀

juvenile

♂

white-eyed race

♂

EASTERN TOWHEE

♂

SPOTTED TOWHEE

BLUE GROSBEAK *Guiraca caerulea* **to 7½"**

VOICE: A rapid warble of short phrases that rise and fall. Call note is a metallic *chink*.

FOOD: A rarity at the winter feeder as most leave the U.S. Oil sunflower seed and peanut hearts. Also oranges.

NOTES: Extending range northward. Stragglers are seen well to the north in the spring and fall.

INDIGO BUNTING *Passerina cyanea* **5½"**

VOICE: A lively jumble of high notes: *set sweet sweet, chew chew, tree tree.*

FOOD: Occasionally will stop in spring and fall migration. Will take Niger thistle and proso millet.

NOTES: Can look black if lit from behind. Rare north to Nova Scotia. Has hybridized with the Lazuli Bunting at western edge of range.

LAZULI BUNTING *Passerina amoena* **to 5½"**

VOICE: Similar to the Indigo's.

FOOD: Stops during migration for sunflower seeds and oranges.

NOTES: Breeds to western edge of territory covered by this book. Its range overlaps with that of the Indigo, and it hybridizes regularly.

PAINTED BUNTING *Passerina ciris* **5⅕"**

VOICE: A pleasant warble. Call note is a *chip*.

FOOD: Will feed at tray or on ground. Proso millet, oil sunflower seed, and oranges.

NOTES: A visually arresting songbird. Casual to New England.

BLUE FINCHES,
etc.

♀

♂

BLUE GROSBEAK

♂ molting

♂ summer

♀

INDIGO BUNTING

♀

♂

LAZULI
BUNTING

♀

♂

PAINTED BUNTING

63

BLACKBIRDS, ORIOLES, etc. Family Icteridae

BOBOLINK *Dolichonyx oryzivorus*   to 8"
VOICE: Clear, bubbling, reedy notes are often given in flight while hovering. Flight note a clear *pink*.
FOOD: Extremely rare at feeder. Takes millet.
NOTES: Population is declining in many areas because of diminishing grasslands and harvesting schedules.

EASTERN MEADOWLARK
Sturnella magna   9"
VOICE: 2 clear, slurred whistles that drop at the end: *tee-yah tee-yair.* Buzzy *dzrrt.*
FOOD: Usually not a feeder bird but in some areas it has shown up to take millet.
NOTES: Numbers are decreasing in many areas because of loss of habitat.

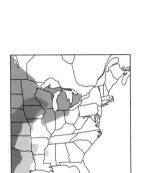

WESTERN MEADOWLARK
Sturnella neglecta   9"
VOICE: 7–10 flutelike and gurgling notes introduced by 1 clear whistle.
FOOD: See Eastern Meadowlark.
NOTES: Although it overlaps with the Eastern Meadowlark, it rarely interbreeds. The eastern range in winter is not well known.

STARLINGS Family Sturnidae

A family of more than 100 species that vary in color from iridescent purples to brilliant oranges and yellows. Highly gregarious. Our one species was introduced from Europe. **FOOD IN WILD:** Everything!

EUROPEAN STARLING
Sturnus vulgaris   to 8½"
VOICE: A jumble of whistles, squeaks, and slurred notes. Occasionally attempts to mimic other birds.
FOOD: Dominates feeders. Do not put out bread. Less likely to come to hanging feeders.
NOTES: A problem species that has impacted native species such as the Eastern Bluebird, from which it takes its nesting hole. Large roosting congregations cause problems.

ICTERIDS,
STARLINGS

BOBOLINK

♀

♂ summer

♂ winter

EASTERN
MEADOWLARK

sexes
similar

WESTERN
MEADOWLARK

sexes
similar

juvenile

winter

summer

EUROPEAN
STARLING

65

OLD WORLD SPARROWS Family Passeridae

Two representatives of an Old World family. Brought to U.S. from England. Not related to native sparrows. **FOOD IN WILD:** Insects and seeds.

HOUSE SPARROW *Passer domesticus*   6"
VOICE: A jumble of unstructured notes. Squeaks, twitters, and whistles.
FOOD: Undesirable, as they flock to feeder and take over. Do not like safflower. Can be limited with screening around feeders.
NOTES: Introduced. Has moved into locales in which humans have modified the environment.

EURASIAN TREE SPARROW
Passer montanus   5³/₅"
VOICE: A repeated *chit-tchup* and a jumble of higher notes. Flight note is a distinct *tek, tek*.
FOOD: Potential problem as population grows. Seeds.
NOTES: Introduced in St. Louis in 1870. Only recently has shown some spreading north into other areas.

GROSBEAKS, FINCHES, SPARROWS, BUNTINGS
Families Fringillidae, Emberizidae, Cardinalidae

DICKCISSEL *Spiza americana*   to 7"
VOICE: A staccato *dick-ciss-ciss-ciss*. A rough buzzing note is heard overhead in migration.
FOOD: Some wander East in fall and winter and may visit feeders. Sunflower seed, millet.
NOTES: Female similar to female House Finch.

LARK BUNTING
Calamospiza melanocorys   7"
VOICE: Cardinal-like slurs, chips, and whistles.
FOOD: Very rare at feeders. Sunflower seed and grains.
NOTES: Sporadic at edges of range. Casual or accidental in East.

FINCHES AND FINCHLIKE BIRDS

HOUSE SPARROW

♂

♀

EURASIAN TREE SPARROW

sexes similar

DICKCISSEL

♂

♀

fall

Bobolink for comparison (see p. 65)

♂ summer

winter ♂ similar to ♀

LARK BUNTING

♀

67

FOX SPARROW *Passerella iliaca* **to 7½"**

VOICE: Musical. A varied arrangement of short clear notes and whistles.

FOOD: Ground or tray feeders. Cracked corn, peanut pieces, oil sunflower seed.

NOTES: A large sparrow that is a winter visitor to brushy areas and feeding stations.

SONG SPARROW *Melospiza melodia* **to 6½"**

VOICE: A series of rollicking notes. Clear notes to start: *Sweet-sweet-sweet,* etc.

FOOD: On ground or tray. Rare to hanging feeder. Cracked corn, millet, oil sunflower seed.

NOTES: Perhaps our most common sparrow. Has a long tail and a dark chest spot.

VESPER SPARROW *Pooecetes gramineus* **6"**

VOICE: Throatier than Song Sparrow. Begins with 2 clear minor notes and then 2 higher ones.

FOOD: Not to be expected at feeder, but when they come, they take millet on the ground.

NOTES: Disappearing from many areas of the Northeast because of loss of grassland habitat.

SAVANNAH SPARROW

Passerculus sandwichensis **to 5⁷⁄₁₀"**

VOICE: A lisping *tsit-tsit-tsit, teeeee-tsaaaay.*

FOOD: Visits feeder mainly in migration or in hard winter. Millet, oil sunflower seed on the ground.

NOTES: Habitat loss is affecting some populations. A numerous sparrow in migration.

STREAKED
SPARROWS

sexes similar

FOX
SPARROW

SONG
SPARROW

VESPER
SPARROW

SWAMP
SPARROW
(see p. 73)

immature

SAVANNAH
SPARROW

Purple
Finch
♀

House
Finch
♀

females for comparison with sparrows
(males shown on p. 47)

69

WHITE-THROATED SPARROW
Zonotrichia albicollis   **to 7"**

VOICE: A clear, pensive, whistled *oh-sweet-sweet-sweet* or a double-parted *oh-sam-pea-body pea-body*. Call note is a hard *chink*.

FOOD: Classic winter feeder sparrow. Ground or tray feeder. Oil sunflower seed, cracked corn, millet, peanut hearts.

NOTES: There are two forms: a white-striped head and a tan-striped head.

WHITE-CROWNED SPARROW
Zonotrichia leucophrys   **to 7½"**

VOICE: A *sweet-sweet-sweet-teedle-de-de deet* that rises at the end.

FOOD: Ground or tray feeder. Sunflower seed, millet.

NOTES: Rarely travels to the southeastern coast.

HARRIS'S SPARROW
Zonotrichia querula   **to 7½"**

VOICE: A quavering song of opening clear whistles on the same pitch, then lower-pitched notes. Alarm note is a *wink* (G. M. Sutton).

FOOD: Takes oil sunflower seed, cracked corn, or millet on the ground or on a tray.

NOTES: This central plains species is rare to the East Coast, where it often visits feeders.

GOLDEN-CROWNED SPARROW
Zonotrichia atricapilla   **to 7"**

This species is a casual to accidental visitor to the East. Most reports are of birds seen at feeding stations from Nova Scotia to Massachusetts. Feeds on the ground on millet and oil sunflower seed.

SPARROWS

WHITE-THROATED SPARROW
tan-striped form

white-striped form

summer
similar in winter

summer
duller in winter

WHITE-CROWNED SPARROW

immature

adult

immature

GOLDEN-CROWNED SPARROW

adult

adult
summer

immature
winter

HARRIS'S SPARROW

71

CHIPPING SPARROW *Spizella passerina* 5"

VOICE: A staccato chipping on 1 pitch.

FOOD: Few may stay in North during winter. Prefers millet on the ground. Will also take mealworms.

NOTES: Prefers to nest in evergreens.

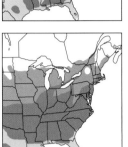

FIELD SPARROW *Spizella pusilla* 5"

VOICE: A series of sweet notes that begins slowly, gains in speed, and ends in a trill.

FOOD: Red and white millet, sunflower pieces on the ground.

NOTES: Often moves about in small groups after nesting season.

SWAMP SPARROW
Melospiza georgiana to 5⁷⁄₁₀"

VOICE: A strong, evenly spaced, rattled trill, at times on 2 pitches. Call note: *chip*.

FOOD: Rare feeder visitor. Takes millet and oil sunflower seed.

NOTES: Distinguish from Song Sparrow by sparsely streaked breast contrasting with whitish throat; gray eyebrow.

AMERICAN TREE SPARROW
Spizella arborea 6"

VOICE: A sweet jumble of notes—often compared to jingling of keys. Call note: *teelwit*.

FOOD: Common winter visitor to feeders. Millet, sunflower seed on tray. Suet.

NOTES: Often forms large winter groups.

RUFOUS-CROWNED SPARROW
Aimophila ruficeps to 6"

VOICE: Stuttering, gurgles. Call note: *dear, dear, dear.*

FOOD: Very rare at feeder. Variety of small seeds.

NOTES: Breeds east locally to e. Oklahoma and w. Arkansas.

RUSTY-CAPPED SPARROWS

sexes similar

winter

summer

CHIPPING SPARROW

juvenile

for comparison
with winter
Chipping Sparrow,
above

juvenile

FIELD SPARROW

CLAY-COLORED SPARROW
(see p. 75)

SWAMP SPARROW

immature

RUFOUS-CROWNED SPARROW

AMERICAN TREE SPARROW

LARK SPARROW

Chondestes grammacus **to 6½"**

VOICE: Clear notes and trills with pauses between them. Buzzy phrases.

FOOD: Rare at feeder. Takes sunflower seed, millet, and cracked corn.

NOTES: Has withdrawn from some breeding areas on eastern edge of range. A rare fall transient to the East Coast.

CLAY-COLORED SPARROW

Spizella pallida **5"**

VOICE: Unbirdlike: 3 or 4 low, flat buzzes: *bzzz, bzzz, bzzz.*

FOOD: Rare at feeder. Takes millet on tray or ground.

NOTES: Pale lores. White mustache stripe. Extending its range eastward. A regular fall transient on the East Coast.

GRASSHOPPER SPARROW

Ammodramus savannarum **to 5"**

VOICE: 2 faint introductory notes followed by high, thin buzz: *tsick, tsick-tiszeeeeeeee.*

FOOD: Very rare at feeders. Millet.

NOTES: Declining in many areas because of loss of grassland nesting habitat.

BACHMAN'S SPARROW

Aimophila aestivalis **5⁷/₁₀"**

VOICE: A clear, liquid whistle followed by a loose trill or warble. (Vaguely suggests Hermit Thrush's song).

FOOD: Rare at feeders. Millet.

NOTES: Disappearing from northern parts of range. Populations are feeling pressure of habitat loss.

SPARROWS
(Mostly clear-breasted)

sexes similar

juvenile

adult

LARK SPARROW

CHIPPING SPARROW
winter

summer

winter

see summer adult on p. 73

CLAY-COLORED SPARROW

GRASSHOPPER SPARROW

adult

BACHMAN'S SPARROW

HENSLOW'S SPARROW

juvenile

75

ORIOLES Family Icteridae

Brightly colored members of the Blackbird family. **FOOD IN WILD:** Insects, spiders, fruit, nectar.

ORCHARD ORIOLE *Icterus spurius*   **to 7"**
VOICE: A fast outburst of clear whistles that bubble to an ending of *wheeer*. Call a soft *chuck*.
FOOD: Less likely than other orioles to visit feeders. Likes oranges and sugar water.
NOTES: Expanding in northern part of its range. First-year males in yellow plumage have black throat.

BALTIMORE ORIOLE *Icterus galbula*   **to 8"**
VOICE: Three clear whistles, then a bubbling *twee-dle-eet-doot*.
FOOD: Loves sugar water and grape jelly. Use weigh-triggered feeders to keep out bees.
NOTES: Its pendulous white nest is a familiar sight. A few winter at northern feeders.

BULLOCK'S ORIOLE
Icterus bullockii   **to 8½"**
VOICE: A series of double notes followed by 1 or 2 piping notes. Also a sharp *skip;* a rough chatter.
FOOD: See Baltimore Oriole. Will also take apple halves.
NOTES: Stragglers occur at feeders in the East in winter.

SPOT-BREASTED ORIOLE
Icterus pectoralis   **8"**
VOICE: A loud, long ensemble of whistles—classicly oriole-like.
FOOD: Will come to sugar water feeders and orange slices.
NOTES: Found only on east coast of Florida. The only spot-breasted oriole in the area.

ORIOLES

ORCHARD ORIOLE

♂

immature ♂

♀

BALTIMORE ORIOLE

♂

immature ♂

♀

BULLOCK'S ORIOLE

♂

♀

SPOT-BREASTED ORIOLE
(Florida only)

♂

♀ similar but duller

THRUSHES Family Turdidae

Large-eyed, slender-billed, round-bodied songbirds. All young have spotted breasts. Excellent singers. **FOOD IN WILD:** Insects, worms, snails, fruit.

EASTERN BLUEBIRD *Sialia sialis*   7"
VOICE: A soft, musical churring and *chur-wi*.
FOOD: Mealworms, raisins. Plantings.
NOTES: This well-known species has benefited from nesting box programs that have led to its recovery in many areas.

MOUNTAIN BLUEBIRD
Sialia currucoides   7"
This rare winter visitor from the West is turquoise blue or grayish with a blue rump and a long bill. Often flutter feeds on fruits or plantings. Attracted to Redcedar Juniper.

AMERICAN ROBIN
Turdus migratorius   to 11"
VOICE: A variety of clear, caroling phrases that rise and fall, especially at dawn and dusk. Call: a soft *tup tup*.
FOOD: Apples, mealworms. Plantings: sumac, cherry, chokecherry. Provide water.
NOTES: Our most familiar songbird. Builds mud-lined nests in tree crotches on flat surfaces.

VARIED THRUSH *Ixoreus naevius*   to 10"
Shown here to compare to American Robin, as this rare visitor from the West appears with some regularity at eastern bird feeders in winter.
FOOD: Sunflower seed, apples. Plantings: Redcedar Juniper.

NORTHERN WHEATEAR
Oenanthe oenanthe   6"
VOICE: A *chack, chack* or *chak-wheet-eeeer*.
FOOD: Does not come to feeders.
NOTES: Autumn stray to East Coast. Visits coastal areas, dunes, and open rocky farmlands.

♀

♂

juvenile

**EASTERN
BLUEBIRD**

♂

**MOUNTAIN
BLUEBIRD**

♂

♀

juvenile

**AMERICAN
ROBIN**

♂

**VARIED
THRUSH**

summer

winter

**NORTHERN
WHEATEAR**

PIGEONS and DOVES Family Columbidae

Trim to plump, fast-flying birds with small heads. Gregarious. Passenger Pigeon is extinct. **FOOD:** Seeds, fruits, grains, cracked corn. Ground feeders. Provide space, as they are not tolerant of other birds close-by. Provide water.

MOURNING DOVE *Zenaida macroura*   12"
VOICE: A mournful, hollow *coah, cooo, coo, coo*. Often mistaken for an owl calling.
FOOD: Ground feeder. Sunflower, sorghum, millet.
NOTES: Pugnacious at feeders.

COMMON GROUND-DOVE
Columbina passerina   6½"
VOICE: A soft, repeated *woo-oo, woo-oo*.
FOOD: Ground feeder. Millet, grass seeds, sorghum.
NOTES: Small, sparrowlike; rusty outerwings. Nods head when it walks. Wanders north on occasion.

INCA DOVE *Columbina inca*   to 7½"
VOICE: A double *coo-coo*.
Now resident in Texas and Louisiana. Very rare wanderer to north. Roadsides, fields, and waste places. Long tail with white edge. Scaled breast.

WHITE-WINGED DOVE *Zenaida asiatica*   11½"
VOICE: A distinct *who cooks for you*.
Wanders to East Coast in fall and winter. Found in West to e. Texas and in Florida. Square tail, large white wing patches.

WHITE-CROWNED PIGEON *Columba leucocephala*   13"
VOICE: A deep, resonant *coo-ka-croo-coo-coo*.
Extreme s. Florida and Keys species. Large, dark with white to grayish crown. Flocks commute inland from offshore nesting islands for fruit.

RINGED TURTLE-DOVE *Streptopelia risoria*   to 12"
VOICE: *Cooo-ka-roo*.
All blond with black neck-ring. Domesticated birds escape on occasion and visit feeders. Formerly established in Florida.

ROCK DOVE (Domestic or Feral Pigeon)
Columba livia   to 13"
VOICE: A gurgling *cooo-kura-coo-coo*.
Perhaps the best-known bird in the U.S. Lives everywhere humans live.

PASSENGER
PIGEON

extinct

PIGEONS, DOVES

sexes similar

COMMON
GROUND-DOVE

INCA
DOVE

MOURNING
DOVE

WHITE-
CROWNED
PIGEON

WHITE-
WINGED
DOVE

plumages
variable

ROCK DOVE
(Domestic or
Feral Pigeon)

RINGED
TURTLE-
DOVE

typical or
ancestral
form

81

HUMMINGBIRDS Family Trochilidae

The smallest birds. Usually iridescent with needlelike bills for sipping nectar. Jewellike throat feathers. Can hover and fly backward. Pugnacious. **NOTE**: In recent years several western species of hummingbirds have shown up at feeders especially along the Gulf Coast. Any hummingbird visiting a feeder after November 1 in the Northeast or during early winter in the South should be carefully checked against the plates in the *Field Guide to Western Birds*. You many find an exciting rarity. **FOOD IN WILD**: Nectar of flowers (red flowers are favored), aphids, and other small insects.

RUBY-THROATED HUMMINGBIRD
Archilochus colubris

3¾" (including bill)

VOICE: In aerial display male flies in pendulum pattern accompanied by hum. Call: squeaks.

FOOD: Takes sugar water from hanging feeders. Attracted to flower gardens with red flowers such as Impatiens.

NOTES: The only common eastern hummingbird. Green to gray sides. Male's ruby throat seen only when the sun's angle is right; otherwise throat looks black.

RUFOUS HUMMINGBIRD
Selasphorus rufus   3½" (including bill)

VOICE: High-pitched chips and twitters.

FOOD: Sugar water in hanging feeders. Also attracted to garden flowers.

NOTES: Look for this visitor from the West in the late fall or early winter at hummingbird feeders or late-flowering Salvia (usually females or immatures). Rusty sides and rust in tail. Other western species may wander to East, especially to Gulf Coast states.

RUBY-THROATED HUMMINGBIRD

Sphinx moth resembles hummingbird

RUFOUS HUMMINGBIRD

WOOD-WARBLERS Family Parulidae

Small, brightly colored, active birds with thin bills. Majority have some yellow in plumage. **FOOD IN WILD:** Mainly insects, spiders, larvae. **NOTE:** These beautiful birds are most familiar to us as migrants in the spring and fall when mixed groups migrate north to breed. During the summer, enough food is available afield and feeders are not needed. Most leave the U.S. to winter on Caribbean Islands or in Cen. America. The following three have appeared consistently at feeders in migration and during winter months.

PINE WARBLER *Dendroica pinus* 5½"
VOICE: A musical, one-pitched trill.
FOOD: When it has visited—suet, oranges, millet, and mealworms.
NOTES: Increasing numbers in New England. Few may winter in the North. Earliest nesting warbler. Local in northern part of range.

YELLOW-RUMPED ("Myrtle") WARBLER
Dendroica coronata 6"
VOICE: A loose jumble of notes that rises in pitch, and drops at the end. Call note, loud *check.*
FOOD: Loves bayberries. Will take mealworms, orange slices, peanut butter mix, and suet.
NOTES: May winter well north. Western form ("Audubon's" Warbler) very rare in East.

ORANGE-CROWNED WARBLER
Vermivora celata to 5"
VOICE: A colorless trill that grows weaker at the end. Often changes in pitch, rising and then dropping.
FOOD: Loves suet, oranges, and mealworms.
NOTES: Seen as a migrant. More sightings occur in the fall. Drab and often overlooked. Casual in winter as far north as Cape Cod.

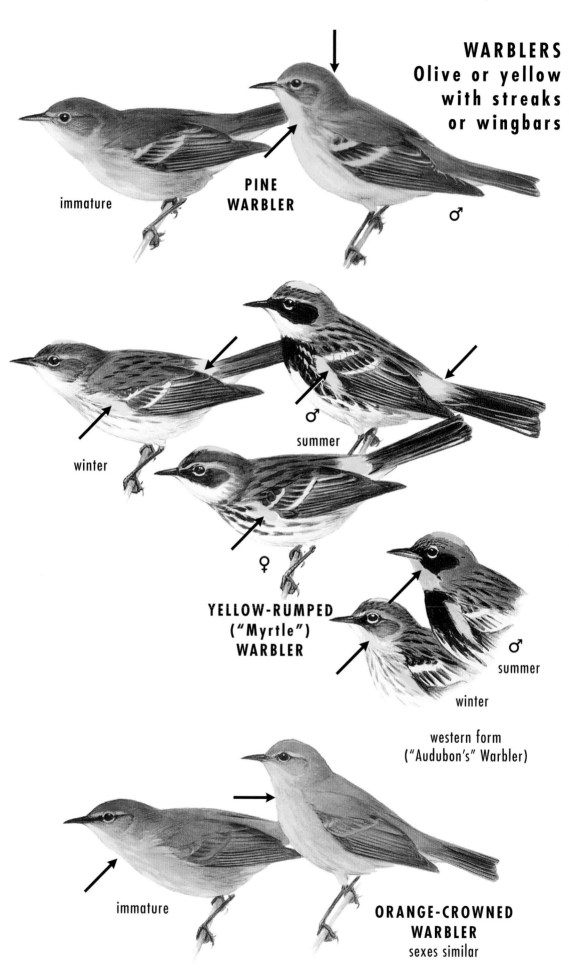

WARBLERS
Olive or yellow
with streaks
or wingbars

immature

PINE
WARBLER

♂

winter

♂
summer

♀

YELLOW-RUMPED
("Myrtle")
WARBLER

♂
summer

winter

western form
("Audubon's" Warbler)

immature

ORANGE-CROWNED
WARBLER
sexes similar

85

SHRIKES Family Laniidae

Songbirds with hook-tipped bills and bird-of-prey behavior. Perch watchfully on treetops and wires and drop on prey, then impale the prey on thorns, barbed wire. **FOOD IN WILD:** Insects, lizards, mice, small birds.

NORTHERN SHRIKE

Lanius excubitor   **to 10"**

VOICE: A succession of harsh, jumbled notes.

AT FEEDERS: Will act as a predator.

NOTES: Light vermiculations (bars) on breast. Moves south sporadically in winter to dash line.

LOGGERHEAD SHRIKE

Lanius ludovicianus   **9"**

VOICE: Repeated harsh, deliberate phrases *queedle-queedle* or *tsurp-tsurp*.

AT FEEDERS: Can act as a predator.

NOTES: Fast disappearing from many areas, especially in Northeast. Reason for decline is unknown.

WAXWINGS Family Bombycillidae

Sleek, crested, gregarious birds with red waxy tips to their secondaries. **FOOD IN WILD:** Berries most of year. Waxwings "hawk" out over water and open areas for insects in summer and fall.

BOHEMIAN WAXWING

Bombycilla garrulus   **8"**

VOICE: A high-pitched, trembling *zreee*.

FOOD: Comes to plantings: Mountain Ash, cherry and apple trees. Raisins at feeders.

NOTES: Sporadically invades in flocks from the Northwest between dash lines. Starlinglike shape in flight.

CEDAR WAXWING

Bombycilla cedrorum   **7"**

VOICE: A high, ethereal, lisped *tssseeeeee*.

FOOD: Plantings: Redcedar Juniper.

NOTES: Tail tip may be orange in immature. Move about in large flocks in fall and winter.

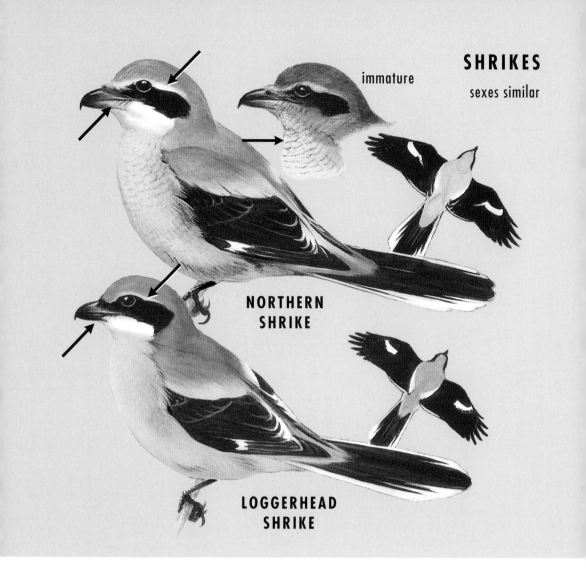

immature

NORTHERN
SHRIKE

LOGGERHEAD
SHRIKE

WAXWINGS

juvenile

♂

♂

BOHEMIAN
WAXWING

CEDAR
WAXWING

CROWS, JAYS, etc. Family Corvidae

Large- to medium-sized birds. Their strong bills are covered with bristles at the base. Sexes look alike. **FOOD IN WILD:** Nearly anything edible.

FISH CROW *Corvus ossifragus* 16" to 20"
VOICE: A nasal, *qua* or *qua-ha*.
FOOD: Will eat most items. Can be a problem if fed bread. Will take young birds.
NOTES: Smaller and trimmer than the American Crow. Fish Crow is best distinguished by its voice.

AMERICAN CROW
Corvus brachyrhynchos 17" to 21"
VOICE: The classic *caw,* plus a wide variety of other guttural sounds. Has its own "language."
FOOD: Cautious but will come into yards. Likes suet, scraps. Will take young birds from nests.
NOTES: One of the best-known wild birds, the American Crow forms winter roosts of thousands.

CHIHUAHUAN RAVEN
Corvus cryptoleucus to 21"
VOICE: A high, hoarse *kraahk*.
FOOD: Not a feeder bird, but on rangeland will come to carcasses or any food item easily available.
NOTES: Barely reaches area covered by this book in Oklahoma, Texas, and Kansas.

COMMON RAVEN *Corvus corax* to 27"
VOICE: A croaking *cr-r-ruck* and a clear *tok*.
FOOD: Feeds on carcasses. Will come to rib cages hung out. Omnivorous.
NOTES: Wedge-shaped tail. Expanding its range.

Fish Crow

FISH
CROW

American
Crow

CHIHUAHUAN
RAVEN

AMERICAN
CROW

Common
Raven

COMMON
RAVEN

TURKEYS Family Meleagrididae

Large fowl. Iridescent feathering, naked head. Male has a "beard" and fans tail in display. **FOOD IN WILD:** Berries, acorns, nuts, seeds, insects.

WILD TURKEY *Meleagris gallopavo*
male to 48", female to 36"

VOICE: A rolling gobble or an alarm *pit*. Female: *keow-keow*.

FOOD: Cracked corn scattered on the ground.

NOTES: One of our most recognizable birds. Populations have increased dramatically in response to restocking efforts. Found locally north to dash line.

PHEASANTS Family Phasianidae (in part)

Chicken-sized ground-dwelling birds. Reluctant to fly. Sexes can be similar or distinctly different. **FOOD IN WILD:** Seeds, berries, buds, insects.

RING-NECKED PHEASANT
Phasianus colchicus
male to 36" (including tail), female to 25"

VOICE: Male: a harsh crowing *kork-kork*. Female: a low clucking.

FOOD: Cracked corn on the ground. Grains. Scratches the ground while feeding.

NOTES: Introduced. Male has a long tail and red face wattles. Female lacks any adornment. This ground nester flushes with an explosive croak.

NORTHERN BOBWHITE
Colinus virginianus **to 10½"**

VOICE: Very familiar, whistled *bob-white* with upward inflection on second note. Covey call is a sharp *whoil-eeeek*.

FOOD: Cracked corn. Likes shelter, such as a lean-to, when feeding.

NOTES: Small, rotund. Heard more often than seen. Explodes into flight when approached too closely. Numbers renewed due to restocking in North.

MISCELLANEOUS
FOWLLIKE BIRDS

display

♂

♂

♀

**WILD
TURKEY**

♂

♀

♀

♀

♂

RING-NECKED PHEASANT

**NORTHERN
BOBWHITE**

♂

♀

91

PREDATORS AT THE FEEDER
HAWKS Family Accipitridae

These long-tailed woodland hawks have short, rounded wings. Typical flight pattern is several beats and a glide. Females are larger. **FOOD IN WILD:** Chiefly birds with some small mammals. Of all the hawks, these three are the ones most often seen hunting at feeders. Provide cover and escape distance around feeders and bird baths.

SHARP-SHINNED HAWK
Accipiter striatus   **to 14"**
VOICE: A high *kik-kik-kik*.
HABITAT: Woods and thickets.
NOTES: Trim body, square tail, and small head. Fast, snappy wingbeats before glide. Very local breeder in the South. Population is increasing. More are staying north with increased activity at feeders.

COOPER'S HAWK *Accipiter cooperii* **to 20"**
VOICE: Rapid *kek, kek, kek* at nest site.
HABITAT: Broken woodlands, and river groves.
NOTES: Has a rounded tail tip, large head, and longer neck and straight-edged leading edge to wing compared to Sharp-shinned. Like Sharp-shinned, a regular at birdfeeding stations. Population is increasing.

NORTHERN GOSHAWK
Accipiter gentilis   **to 26"**
VOICE: A sharp, loud *kak, kak, kak* or *kuk, kuk, kuk*. Tenaciously defends nest site.
HABITAT: Evergreen forests and deciduous woods.
NOTES: Large powerful hawk. Long tail. Undertail coverts often wrap up to give white rump appearance. Strong eye stripe. Population is increasing, especially in the Northeast. Takes prey as large as pheasant.

ACCIPITERS, HARRIERS

ACCIPITERS (True Hawks) have small heads, short, rounded wings, and long tails

immature

adult

SHARP-SHINNED HAWK

COOPER'S HAWK

immature

adult

immature

adult

NORTHERN GOSHAWK

Northern Harrier

immature

♂

♀

NORTHERN HARRIER

TANAGERS Family Thraupidae

Male tanagers are brightly colored; females are olive green above, yellowish below. Thick bills. Mainly tropical birds. A few species reach the U.S. **FOOD IN WILD:** Insects, fruit.

SUMMER TANAGER *Piranga rubra* **to 7⁷/₁₀"**
VOICE: Call note is a staccato *pik-i-tuk-i-tuk*. Song is robinlike and clear; questioning.
FOOD: Rare at winter feeders in Northeast. Trays or off-ground feeders. Will take suet, raisins, fruit, sunflower seeds.
NOTES: Casual in spring as far north as Nova Scotia. Rarely seen at winter feeders.

SCARLET TANAGER *Piranga olivacea* **7"**
VOICE: A raspy, see-sawing *tweer, tawoo, tweer*. Call note *chip-burrr*.
FOOD: Extremely rare in winter. Might stop for oranges and raisins during migration.
NOTES: Males in changing plumage have blotches of red or orange.

WESTERN TANAGER *Piranga ludoviciana* **7"**
A western species that very rarely wanders east. Records into Canada. Comes to winter feeders when out of range. Takes suet, raisins, seed. Use care in identification, as young Scarlet Tanagers can have a thin yellowish wingbar. Check for dusky saddleback appearance.

BLUE-GRAY TANAGER
Thraupis episcopus **6"**
Shown here based on a population that at one time was established in and around Hollywood, Florida. There have been no recent sightings.

TANAGERS

SUMMER
TANAGER

♀

♂ *all seasons*

immature
changing to
adult

SCARLET
TANAGER

♀

♂ *changing*

♂ *summer*

♂ *winter*

♂ *orange
variant*

WESTERN
TANAGER

♀

♂ *summer*

♂ *winter*

BLUE-GRAY
TANAGER
sexes similar

95

PARROTS, PARAKEETS Family Psittacidae

Compact, short-necked birds with stout, hooked bills. Noisy. Carolina Parakeet was the only native parakeet to occur in e. U.S. Now extinct, it was last reported in 1920 in Florida. A number of exotic species have been released or escaped; several species have established themselves. **FOOD IN WILD:** Fruits and all seeds; cracked corn. Ground feeders. At feeders, large numbers can be damaging and loud. They often rip away at feeders with powerful bills, damaging or destroying them.

MONK PARAKEET *Myiopsitta monachus* 11½"
VOICE: Raucous squawking.

Long tail and gray hood are distinct. From Argentina. Released into Florida, the Northeast, and the Midwest, where it has become established. The only parrot to build a stick nest (all others nest in holes), it prefers to build in conifers. Can damage fruit. Raucous noise in nesting colonies.

WHITE-WINGED PARAKEET *Brotogeris versicolurus* 9"
VOICE: Strident, loud screams.

Long tail and bright white and yellow wing patches. Well established (numbers in the hundreds) only in Florida, but escapes have been recorded as far north as Mass.

BUDGERIGAR *Melopsittacus undulatus* to 7"
VOICE: Squawks and cackles. In flocks screams loudly.

Familar to all, the green form is the true color of this Australian native. Declining resident in Florida. Pet escapes seen as far north as New England.

The following species have been seen with some regularity as escapes and could show up at feeders. Native in sites listed.
1. Yellow-headed Parrot. *Amazona oratrix.* Tropical America.
2. Black-hooded Conure (Nanday Conure). *Nandayus nenday.* S. America.
3. Blossom-headed Parakeet. *Psittacula roseata.* Himalayas.
4. Ring-necked Parakeet. *Psittacula krameri.* India.
5. Yellow-collared Lovebird. *Agapornis personatus.* E. Africa.
6. Hispaniolan Parakeet. *Aratinga chloroptera.* Hispaniola.
7. Green Parakeet. *Aratinga holochlora.* Mexico.
8. Red-crowned Parrot. *Amazona viridigenalis.* Mexico.
9. Orange-fronted Parakeet. *Aratinga canicularis.* Mexico.
10. Orange-chinned Parakeet. *Brotogeris jugularis.* Cen. America.
11. Cockatiel. *Nymphicus hollandicus.* Australia.

CAROLINA PARAKEET
(formerly endemic,
now extinct)

PARROTS (Escapes)

WHITE-
WINGED
PARAKEET

MONK
PARAKEET

BUDGERIGAR
Some individuals
may be blue or yellow

OCCASIONAL ESCAPES

1

2

3

4

5

6

7

8

9

10

11

FEEDER CHECKLIST

SPECIES	YEARS						NOTES
	06	07	08	09	10	11	
Blackbird, Brewer's	✓	—	—	—	—	—	*Arrived in Snowstorm*
Blackbird, Brewer's	—	—	—	—	—	—	
Blackbird, Red-winged	—	—	—	—	—	—	
Blackbird, Rusty	—	—	—	—	—	—	
Blackbird, Yellow-headed	—	—	—	—	—	—	
Bluebird, Eastern	—	—	—	—	—	—	
Bluebird, Mountain	—	—	—	—	—	—	
Bobolink	—	—	—	—	—	—	
Bobwhite, Northern	—	—	—	—	—	—	
Budgerigar	—	—	—	—	—	—	
Bunting, Indigo	—	—	—	—	—	—	
Bunting, Lark	—	—	—	—	—	—	
Bunting, Lazuli	—	—	—	—	—	—	
Bunting, Painted	—	—	—	—	—	—	
Bunting, Snow	—	—	—	—	—	—	
Cardinal, Northern	—	—	—	—	—	—	
Catbird, Gray	—	—	—	—	—	—	
Chickadee, Black-capped	—	—	—	—	—	—	
Chickadee, Boreal	—	—	—	—	—	—	
Chickadee, Carolina	—	—	—	—	—	—	
Cowbird, Brown-headed	—	—	—	—	—	—	
Creeper, Brown	—	—	—	—	—	—	
Crossbill, Red	—	—	—	—	—	—	
Crossbill, White-winged	—	—	—	—	—	—	
Crow, American	—	—	—	—	—	—	
Crow, Fish	—	—	—	—	—	—	
Dickcissel	—	—	—	—	—	—	
Dove, Common Ground	—	—	—	—	—	—	

SPECIES	YEARS						NOTES
	06	07	08	09	10	11	
Dove, Inca	—	—	—	—	—	—	___
Dove, Mourning	—	—	—	—	—	—	___
Dove, Ringed Turtle	—	—	—	—	—	—	___
Dove, Rock	—	—	—	—	—	—	___
Finch, House	—	—	—	—	—	—	___
Finch, Purple	—	—	—	—	—	—	___
Flicker, Northern	—	—	—	—	—	—	___
Goldfinch, American	—	—	—	—	—	—	___
Grackle, Boat-tailed	—	—	—	—	—	—	___
Grackle, Common	—	—	—	—	—	—	___
Grackle, Great-tailed	—	—	—	—	—	—	___
Grosbeak, Black-headed	—	—	—	—	—	—	___
Grosbeak, Blue	—	—	—	—	—	—	___
Grosbeak, Evening	—	—	—	—	—	—	___
Grosbeak, Pine	—	—	—	—	—	—	___
Grosbeak, Rose-breasted	—	—	—	—	—	—	___
Hummingbird, Ruby-throated	—	—	—	—	—	—	___
Hummingbird, Rufous	—	—	—	—	—	—	___
Jay, Blue	—	—	—	—	—	—	___
Jay, Florida Scrub-	—	—	—	—	—	—	___
Jay, Gray	—	—	—	—	—	—	___
Junco, Dark-eyed	—	—	—	—	—	—	___
Kinglet, Golden-crowned	—	—	—	—	—	—	___
Kinglet, Ruby-crowned	—	—	—	—	—	—	___
Magpie, Black-billed	—	—	—	—	—	—	___
Martin, Purple	—	—	—	—	—	—	___
Meadowlark, Eastern	—	—	—	—	—	—	___
Meadowlark, Western	—	—	—	—	—	—	___
Mockingbird, Northern	—	—	—	—	—	—	___
Nuthatch, Brown-headed	—	—	—	—	—	—	___
Nuthatch, Red-breasted	—	—	—	—	—	—	___
Nuthatch, White-breasted	—	—	—	—	—	—	___
Oriole, Baltimore	—	—	—	—	—	—	___
Oriole, Bullock's	—	—	—	—	—	—	___
Oriole, Orchard	—	—	—	—	—	—	___
Oriole, Spot-breasted	—	—	—	—	—	—	___

SPECIES	YEARS						NOTES
	06	07	08	09	10	11	
Parakeet, Monk	—	—	—	—	—	—	
Parakeet, White-winged	—	—	—	—	—	—	
Pheasant, Ring-necked	—	—	—	—	—	—	
Pigeon, White-crowned	—	—	—	—	—	—	
Raven, Chihuahuan	—	—	—	—	—	—	
Raven, Common	—	—	—	—	—	—	
Redpoll, Common	—	—	—	—	—	—	
Redpoll, Hoary	—	—	—	—	—	—	
Robin, American	—	—	—	—	—	—	
Sapsucker, Yellow-bellied	—	—	—	—	—	—	
Siskin, Pine	—	—	—	—	—	—	
Solitaire, Townsend's	—	—	—	—	—	—	
Sparrow, American Tree	—	—	—	—	—	—	
Sparrow, Bachman's	—	—	—	—	—	—	
Sparrow, Chipping	—	—	—	—	—	—	
Sparrow, Clay-colored	—	—	—	—	—	—	
Sparrow, Eurasian Tree	—	—	—	—	—	—	
Sparrow, Field	—	—	—	—	—	—	
Sparrow, Fox	—	—	—	—	—	—	
Sparrow, Golden-crowned	—	—	—	—	—	—	
Sparrow, Grasshopper	—	—	—	—	—	—	
Sparrow, Harris's	—	—	—	—	—	—	
Sparrow, Henslow's	—	—	—	—	—	—	
Sparrow, House	—	—	—	—	—	—	
Sparrow, Lark	—	—	—	—	—	—	
Sparrow, Rufous-crowned	—	—	—	—	—	—	
Sparrow, Savannah	—	—	—	—	—	—	
Sparrow, Song	—	—	—	—	—	—	
Sparrow, Swamp	—	—	—	—	—	—	
Sparrow, Vesper	—	—	—	—	—	—	
Sparrow, White-crowned	—	—	—	—	—	—	
Sparrow, White-throated	—	—	—	—	—	—	
Starling, European	—	—	—	—	—	—	
Tanager, Scarlet	—	—	—	—	—	—	
Tanager, Summer	—	—	—	—	—	—	
Tanager, Western	—	—	—	—	—	—	

SPECIES	YEARS						NOTES
	06	07	08	09	10	11	
Thrasher, Brown	—	—	—	—	—	—	_____
Thrush, Varied	—	—	—	—	—	—	_____
Titmouse, Tufted	—	—	—	—	—	—	_____
Towhee, Eastern	—	—	—	—	—	—	_____
Towhee, Green-tailed	—	—	—	—	—	—	_____
Towhee, Spotted	—	—	—	—	—	—	_____
Turkey, Wild	—	—	—	—	—	—	_____
Warbler, Orange-crowned	—	—	—	—	—	—	_____
Warbler, Pine	—	—	—	—	—	—	_____
Warbler, Yellow-rumped	—	—	—	—	—	—	_____
Waxwing, Bohemian	—	—	—	—	—	—	_____
Waxwing, Cedar	—	—	—	—	—	—	_____
Woodpecker, Black-backed	—	—	—	—	—	—	_____
Woodpecker, Downy	—	—	—	—	—	—	_____
Woodpecker, Hairy	—	—	—	—	—	—	_____
Woodpecker, Pileated	—	—	—	—	—	—	_____
Woodpecker, Red-bellied	—	—	—	—	—	—	_____
Woodpecker, Red-cockaded	—	—	—	—	—	—	_____
Woodpecker, Red-headed	—	—	—	—	—	—	_____
Woodpecker, Three-toed	—	—	—	—	—	—	_____
Wren, Bewick's	—	—	—	—	—	—	_____
Wren, Carolina	—	—	—	—	—	—	_____
Wren, House	—	—	—	—	—	—	_____
Wren, Winter	—	—	—	—	—	—	_____

INDEX

All birds illustrated and described in this book are indexed. The page number(s), with rare exception, refer(s) to the text; it is understood that the illustration is on the right-hand facing page. Scientific names (in *italics*) are keyed to the pages on which the text appears, not the illustrations.